D1567352

AMTRAK
Trains & Travel

Train 8, the North Coast Hiawatha, slams by the St. Paul yard on a very cold January, 1979 Sunday afternoon. Delivered to the Milwaukee Road three hours late by the Burlington Northern, the Milwaukee will endeavor to make up some time over its 419 miles of the train's transcontinental run from Seattle to Chicago. If one is questionning the train number, the North Coast runs as trains 7 and 8 between Chicago and St. Paul, and as 17 and 18 between St. Paul and Seattle. (Patrick C. Dorin and Russ Isbrandt).

AMTRAK
Trains & Travel

By Patrick Dorin

Superior PUBLISHING COMPANY

Library of Congress Cataloging in Publication Data

Dorin, Patrick C.
   Amtrack trains and travel.

   Bibliography: p.
   Includes index.
   SUMMARY: A review of Amtrak's history, services, accommodations, and problems.
   1. Amtrak. [1. Amtrak. 2. Railroads] I. Title.
TF25.A57D67   385'.22'0973   79-22566
ISBN 0-87564-533-X

FIRST EDITION

Photographic reproduction by Artcraft Colorgraphics—Seattle, WA.

Printed and bound in the United States of America

Table of Contents

FORWARD

A Metroliner cuts through the night with its headlight beam at 110 miles per hour— The Southwest Limited charges through the Kansas prairie with three SDP-40F's at 90 miles per hour.— A group of skiers sing songs and play musical instruments as the Montrealer works its way north to Vermont during a snowy New England winter night. These are some of the scenes of Amtrak, the Nation's Rail Passenger train service.

Amtrak is the organization that was put together to save a crucial mode of public transport, a form of transportation that was ailing badly under the private railroad operation. Some say that Amtrak was to be the instrument to finally put the passenger train in the museum, along with the stage coach and other early forms of transportation, however excessive highway and air transport costs and a realization that the world has a finite supply of petroleum changed all of that. Rail passenger service is now becoming increasingly recognized as a crucial element in a balanced transportation system.

The purpose of this book is to review Amtrak's short history, train services and accommodations and some of the severe problems as well as some of the recommendations for the future both in word and picture. It is hoped that the book will provide the reader with greater insights into Amtrak services as well as the problems of not only the rail passenger service, but of the entire industry.

Patrick C. Dorin

March 1, 1979

Dedicated To
Franklin and Sandra Schnick

ACKNOWLEDGEMENTS

Many, many people assisted this writer with materials, photographs and other data and information during the past four years.

Mr. Joseph Salisbury was responsible for the layout and the production of the actual book.

Karen Dorin Reviewed materials and read and reread much of the manuscript for errors and other types of problems.

Mr. Jim Perske assisted with the selection and production of countless photographs.

Dr. Russel B. Adams of the University of Minnesota provided the writer with much encouragement and advice, as the book actually began as a project for the Department of Geography.

Mr. Jim Scribbins, Mr. Russel Porter and Dr. Russ Isbrandt provided the author with technical data and information concerning various types of passenger equipment.

Mr. James Bryant and his staff in Amtrak's Washington offices provided the writer with not only photographs, but substantial information and data for the manuscript and provided opportunities for field trips to study facilities, equipment and trains. Mr. Bob Casey and Ms. Pam Dickson of the Chicago offices also provided the writer with a substantial amount of time as well as materials for this book. The writer also came in contact with numerous train crews and other Amtrak personnel, who were most cooperative in every way.

Mr. Charles Rogers critiqued the manuscript and made a number of recommendations concerning the presentation.

The following organizations, magazines or journals and companies were kind enough to permit use of their materials and other published information: The Budd Company, Southern Railway, the California Department of Transportation, Richard D. Irwin, Incorporated (publishers), *Traffic World, Modern Railroads,* and the National Association of Railroad Passengers.

The following individuals assisted the writer with photographs for the book: Mr. J.W. Swanberg, Mr. James Morin, Mr. David J. Balzer, Mr. A. Robert Johnson, Dr. Robert Clark, Mr. Harold Zabel, Mr. Richard H. Kindig, Michael and Thomas Dorin.

The author is most grateful to these men and women, who gave freely of their time and energy to the project. Without their kind assistance, the book simply could not have been completed. Should an acknowledgement have been left out inadvertently, this writer trusts it will be found in its appropriate place within the book.

Chapter 1
Introduction

The American Railroads have been in existence for just over 150 years as of this writing in early 1979. In many cases, the industry has dominated the scene for many families throughout the United States and Canada. In many ways, the railroad passenger business peaked out in the late 1920's when the U.S. roads operated some 20,000 passenger trains and carried 77% of the intercity traffic by public mode. The bus lines carred about 15% while the airlines served an almost immeasureably small number.

During the 1930's and 40's, the railroads lost nearly half of the passenger business, and more than 50% of the trains were discontinued by the 1950's. Meanwhile, bus traffic increased to nearly 38% and the airlines' share rose to 14% of the total intercity travel by public mode.

From 1950 to 1970, the railroad's share dropped still further to a total of 7.2% of the commercial share. Of the approximately 450 trains still operating in 1970, 100 were in the process of being discontinued. It was truly a dark hour for U.S. railroading, and for the transportation industry in general, for the nation was far removed from a balanced transportation system.

With such an imbalance, and the fact that the U.S. could not continue the massive construction of highways and airports to meet transportation needs, a proposal was made to create a national rail passenger system. This proposal was viewed not only as a method to save an alternate form of transportation, but also because rail facilities can be upgraded quite economically when compared to the costs of construction of new highways and airports.

The Rail Passenger Service Act was enacted by Congress on October 30,1970. The Board of Incorporators were appointed by President Nixon and they began work on January 1, 1971, just four months before Amtrak would be responsible for the nation's railroad passenger service. May 1st was the day a new chapter in U.S. railroading began, and it is safe to say that Amtrak has been a controversial subject ever since.

There are many controversial subjects in the United States. Some are extremely important and literally represent a life and death struggle for some people while others can produce substantial amounts of emotion with little or no effect on anybody. Amtrak, as a controversial subject, fits somewhere in the middle of these two extremes and is slowly moving to the more serious as time goes on.

Rail passenger service is a complex problem in North America. What is presently happening with Amtrak, is a microcosm of the entire railroad industry, with one difference. Amtrak is being run with government funds, which is natural in view of the fact that it was started by the Federal government.

Amtrak is facing heavy problems. There is an outright campaign being waged to totally destroy the rail passenger system. Although not so obvious, the same thing is happening with the rest of the industry. In those areas where rail transport can excell, there are groups working to prevent it. For example, the Burlington Northern is currently (1978) facing the problem of cities and towns who do not wish to have coal trains rolling through.

During the past 75 years, the railroad industry has had a great deal of difficulty changing laws, improving the unequal taxation, securing greater rate making freedom, and service improvements or changes. Basically this has come about because the public does not understand the railroad problem. This problem prevents Amtrak from doing its best, since not only do the bus companies seem to be after a complete elimination of Amtrak, but the U.S. Department of Transportation and the Office of Management and Budget (in 1978) have been out to cut off all but the heart of the Amtrak System.

The public does not fully understand the complexities of the situation, and consequently government in turn does not understand, and responds only to crisis situations.

The problem is a two edged sword. As of 1978, the railroad industry's exposure to the public is basically Amtrak. When Amtrak fails at something such as late trains or discourteous train crews, the public often feels that it is the railroad industry that is at fault. Prior to Amtrak, one could blame an individual line, but not anymore. Consequently, it is to the railroad industry's benefit that Amtrak flourish and prosper. It is the only way the industry can put its best foot forward for the public. The railroads must seriously take note of this.

U.S. highways are approaching a deplorable state of condition for a variety of reasons, including a lack of appropriate maintenance. After a certain point is reached, the only way to provide a long term solution is to tear up the old pavement completely and start all over. This particular highway is getting the treatment and is receiving an entirely new base. Later, black top will be laid down. A point to remember is that trucks, particularly oveloaded vehicles, do far more damage to the roads than automobiles.

These signs are becoming more and more prevalent throughout the U.S. on all types of roads, including the interstate system. The amount of money that would be spent totally revamping our public transporation is a drop in the bucket compared to what must be spent rebuilding our highways.

If rail travelers are pleased, and word does indeed get passed around, perhaps the public will take the industry more seriously.

Therefore, the U.S. and Canada have a serious problem. The problem is not simply that the traveling public has abandoned the train as a means of travel. If it were only that simple!

The real problem is a lack of understanding of economics by many citizens of both countries, and in particular transportation economics by government leaders. Consequently poor decisions are made, not only based on poor and misrepresented data, but also for favors to groups or individuals on a short run basis, which in turn is often disastrous to the nation as well as the group or individual on a long run basis. Consequently, the problem is one of a fear of and a complete misunderstanding of the real situation in terms of public passenger transportation. Further, and even more seriously, when correct data is ignored by the decision makers, (for whatever reason), then it becomes even more difficult to correct a situation. Eventually, more time and energy as well as money must be used to correct the situation, which must indeed happen.

The current situation in the United States produces even a further question. If the passenger train is so vital to the transportation picture, why then, are so many groups out to eliminate it altogether?

BUS/TRAK II

BUS/TRAK II offers a convenient new Indian Trails Chieftan express bus service along the route of Amtrak's Blue Water Limited. From Chicago our new service provides a convenient evening departure from Amtrak's Chicago Union Station to Kalamazoo, Battle Creek, Lansing/East Lansing, Flint and Saginaw. (Amtrak personnel are available in Union Station to direct you to the proper BUS/TRAK boarding area) If you're headed in the other direction, our Chicago bound BUS/TRAK II offers late afternoon Chieftan express bus service along the same route directly to Chicago Union Station in time to connect with Amtrak's "Empire Builder" and "North Coast Hiawatha" bound for Minneapolis, Spokane and Seattle and Amtrak's "Floridian" bound for Louisville, Birmingham, Jacksonville, Orlando, Tampa/St. Petersburg and Miami.

When you travel on BUS/TRAK II you can use either a standard Indian Trails ticket or an Amtrak standard fare or family plan ticket. (USA Rail Pass, Excursion and Employee Pass tickets are not good for travel on BUS/TRAK II)

Both Indian Trails and Amtrak offer you a relaxing and inexpensive way to travel from city center to city center. When you climb aboard a modern Indian Trails Chieftan bus or an Amtrak Turboliner or Amfleet train you'll discover soft reclining seats with plenty of legroom, a modern climate control system that keeps you warm in the winter and cool in the summer and big picture windows so you can see the sights of Michigan in style.

For more information on our BUS/TRAK II service, call or see an Indian Trails or Amtrak ticket agent or your travel agent.

• •

To find out more about Michigan's new BUS/TRAK services, contact one of the participating rail or bus carriers or write:

Inter City Service Development Section/UPTRAN
Michigan Dept. of State Highways & Transportation
P. O. Box 30050
Lansing, Michigan 48909

BUS/TRAK II

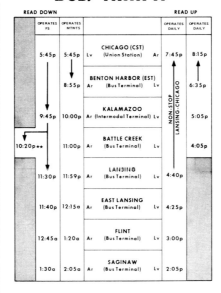

OPERATES FS	OPERATES MTWTS				OPERATES DAILY	OPERATES DAILY
5:45p	5:45p	Lv	CHICAGO (CST) (Union Station)	Ar	7:45p	8:15p
	8:55p	Ar	BENTON HARBOR (EST) (Bus Terminal)	Lv		6:35p
9:45p	10:00p	Ar	KALAMAZOO (Intermodal Terminal)	Lv		5:05p
10:20p**	11:00p	Ar	BATTLE CREEK (Bus Terminal)	Lv		4:05p
11:30p	11:59p	Ar	LANSING (Bus Terminal)	Lv	4:40p	
11:40p	12:15a	Ar	EAST LANSING (Bus Terminal)	Lv	4:25p	
12:45a	1:20a	Ar	FLINT (Bus Terminal)	Lv	3:00p	
1:30a	2:05a	Ar	SAGINAW (Bus Terminal)	Lv	2:05p	

(NON-STOP LANSING-CHICAGO)

FS — Operates on this schedule on Fridays and Sundays.

MTWTS — Operates on this schedule on Mondays, Tuesdays, Wednesdays, Thursdays and Saturdays.

** On FS eastbound passengers bound for Battle Creek change buses in Kalamazoo.

Eastbound service will discharge passengers "On Demand" at the East Lansing Amtrak station. Passengers must inform driver prior to departure from the Lansing bus terminal.

When traveling to Chicago Union Station, passengers must inform driver when boarding the BUS/TRAK coach if they wish to be discharged at Union Station.

Bus/Trak Terminals and Information Guide

The information listed below provides locations and information phone numbers for communities with BUS/TRAK service or with connections to BUS/TRAK service. Personnel at these terminals can provide you with the latest information on fares, routings, schedules, terminal parking availability and other services. It's always a good idea to check with carriers for the latest information before you travel.

● BUS TERMINALS ●

CHICAGO, ILL.
Clark and Randolph Sts.
Information (312) 346-5000

BENTON HARBOR, Mi.
202 Ninth St.
Information (616) 925-1121

KALAMAZOO, Mi.
Intermodal Rail/Bus
459 North Burdick
Information (616) 343-2501

BATTLE CREEK, Mi.
(2 Blocks from Rail Depot)
85 North Division
Information (616) 963-1537

GRAND RAPIDS, Mi.
25 Market St. N. W.
Information (616) 456-1707

LANSING, Mi.
511 S. Washington Ave.
Information (517) 482-0673

EAST LANSING, Mi.
(Serves Mich. State Univ.)
308 W. Grand River
Information (517) 332-2569

JACKSON, Mi.
1414 N. West Ave.
Information (517) 789-6148

FLINT, Mi.
524 North Saginaw
Information (313) 232-1114

SAGINAW, Mi.
511 Johnson St.
Information (517) 753-5454

LAPEER, Mi.
579 West Genesee
Information (313) 664-9113

IMLAY CITY, Mi.
105 Cedar Street
Information (313) 724-4435

PORT HURON, Mi.
315 Pine Street
Information (313) 985-7151

● RAIL TERMINALS ●

CHICAGO, Union Station
210 South Canal (AMTRAK)

KALAMAZOO, Mi.
459 N. Burdick (AMTRAK)

BATTLE CREEK, Mi.
55 W. Van Burren St. (AMTRAK)

LANSING/EAST LANSING, Mi.
1240 South Harrison (AMTRAK)

SARNIA, Ontario (VIA Rail Canada)
South end of Russel St.
Information (519) 344-3657

AMTRAK provides 24 hour per day information on Amtrak and VIA Rail Canada train services through its Toll Free Information Center. If you live in Michigan or Indiana dial 1-(800)-621-0353, Chicago area dial (312)-786-1333, Outstate Illinois dial (800)-972-9147, Ontario dial (800)-263-8130. Additional information on local train service is available by calling the local Amtrak station nearest you. These station numbers are listed in each community's phone book. For VIA Rail Canada information in Toronto dial (416)-367-4300. If you experience trouble dialing any number, ask your operator to assist you.

The State of Michigan has made substantial progress in providing inter-modal service, and both the bus companies and Amtrak have benefited substantially, not to mention the greater conveniences to the traveling public. This folder illustrates the State's efforts that has been appropriately named "Bus-Trak".

Part of the answer is fear. Part of the bus industry seems to be afraid that Amtrak will put them out of business. When one is truly afraid, one does not operate on a rational basis. Blaming Amtrak for traffic losses and annual declines is an easy way to explain away poor service and other problems to the stock holder, the public and the government. This is particularly vexing when one realizes Amtrak does not even compete on most of the bus routes.

Further, some bus companies are trying to lend credibility to their need for survival by explaining that buses are the most efficient mode of transport. According to Greyhound, in 1977 the bus company attained 130 passenger miles per gallon, whereas Amtrak attained only 41 passenger miles per gallon.[1] These figures were based on passengers actually carried by the two companies.

On the surface this looks like the bus system is indeed the more efficient mode of passenger transportation. However, this is only half of the truth. What about the other half of the story? It turns out that a modern Amfleet train can secure up to 500 seat miles per gallon as compared to 265 seat miles for the bus.[2] (See chart in this chapter)

The truth of the matter is that the train is more efficient for larger loads, i.e., five cars or more. For example, at 18 cars the efficiency is about 500 seat miles per gallon. Consequently, in an energy short world the train can carry more people for less fuel than the bus. *This points out that the bus can and should be used for low passenger loads, and the train for heavier traffic and higher speeds in the transportation scheme of things. Each mode has an important role to play.*

In still another report, according to Amtrak, issued by the Energy Research and Development

BUS/TRAK III

Valley Coach Lines, Indian Trails and VIA Rail Canada have teamed up to provide international travelers with an inexpensive and convenient new way to travel between Chicago, Lansing, Flint, Port Huron and Toronto. We call our new intermodal service "BUS/TRAK III".

Here's how it works. Everyday Indian Trails offers Chieftan express bus service between downtown Chicago, Lansing/East Lansing, and Flint. In Flint these buses make direct connections with modern Valley Coach Lines bus service to and from the Sarnia, Ontario VIA Rail Canada train station. Both Indian Trails and Valley Coach offer through ticketing and checked baggage service to make your Flint transfer as easy as stepping off one bus and on to the other. In Sarnia the Valley Coach Lines bus makes direct connections with VIA passenger trains to and from London and Toronto.

If you're bound for eastern Canada, you'll find convenient VIA train connections in Toronto for Ottawa, Montreal, Quebec City and Canada's scenic Maritime Provinces. If you're headed for Chicago, our new service will take you directly to Amtrak's Chicago Union Station in time to connect with evening trains departing to Minneapolis and the Pacific Northwest and to Louisville, Birmingham and points throughout Florida.

To find out more about our new international BUS/TRAK III service, simply call Valley Coach Lines, Indian Trails or VIA Rail Canada. Bus and rail terminal locations and information phone numbers are listed on the reverse side of this folder. For information in the United States on VIA Rail Canada train service throughout Canada, call either VIA or call Amtrak's Toll Free Information Center.

The schedules and services shown in this brochure are subject to change without notice. Service patterns demand that rail and bus connections cannot be guaranteed.

BUS/TRAK III

READ DOWN				READ UP	
2:00a	Lv	CHICAGO (CST) (Bus Terminal)	Ar	7:50p*	
7:10a	Lv	KALAMAZOO (EST) (Intermodal Terminal)	Ar		
9:05a	Lv	LANSING (Bus Terminal)	Ar	4:35p	
9:15a	Lv	EAST LANSING (Bus Terminal)	Ar	4:00p	
10:45a	Ar	FLINT (Bus Terminal)	Lv	3:00p	
10:50a	Lv	FLINT (Bus Terminal)	Ar	2:55p	
11:30a	Lv	LAPEER (Bus Terminal)	Ar	2:15p	
11:50a	Lv	IMLAY CITY (Bus Terminal)	Ar	1:55p	
12:30p	Lv	PORT HURON (Bus Terminal)	Ar	1:15p	
12:45p	Ar	SARNIA (Rail Terminal)	Lv	12:45p	
1:35p	Lv	SARNIA (Rail Terminal)	Ar	12:20p	
2:40p	Ar	LONDON (Rail Terminal)	Lv	11:15a	
5:10p	Lv	TORONTO (Rail Terminal)	Lv	9:00a	

INDIAN TRAILS — VALLEY COACH — VIA (left side); INDIAN TRAILS NON STOP — VALLEY COACH — VIA (right side)

*Indian Trails service bound to Chicago will discharge passengers "ON REQUEST" at Chicago Union Train Station. Passengers must inform driver when boarding the BUS/TRAK coach if they wish to be discharged at Union Station.

Valley Coach service between Flint and Sarnia operates daily except Christmas Day, New Years Day, Easter and Thanksgiving Day. All other services indicated operate daily.

BUS/TRAK III service makes direct connections in Lansing with Greyhound express bus service to and from Grand Rapids and in East Lansing with North Star bus service to and from Jackson. Both transfers offer through ticketing and checked baggage service.

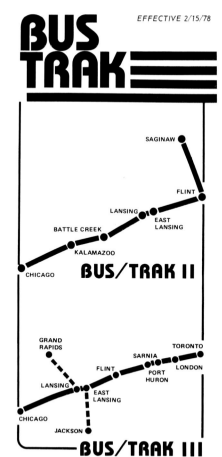

EFFECTIVE 2/15/78

Administration in October, 1976, it was shown that the following BTU's (British Thermal Units) were consumed per seat-mile:[3]

Mode	BTU/Seat-Mile
Metroliner	440
Rail, diesel	583
Bus	1192
Air	2600

The figures speak for themselves.

The other area in which some of the bus companies are attacking Amtrak is the so called subsidy. The American Bus Association has commented that it is not fair to subsidize Amtrak when the bus industry is not subsidized.[4] In many ways, this argument is almost too ludicrous to take seriously.

Some of the bus companies claim that the industry must compete with a mode that is federally funded, and is in fact, destroying the private enterprise system of the bus companies. This is indeed interesting. The expressways and highways are provided by public expense because since 1920

over $150 billion have been spent on the U.S. highways from non-highway revenue sources.[5] The bus lines use these roads and furthermore when the roads decay, the companies literally give up servicing those cities and towns whose roads are not up to standard.

Not only has the government given dollars outright to the highway industry, but also over $40 billion to the airlines and airports since 1920. As of 1979, the subsidy to the air passenger transportation system in the U.S. is exceeding $3 billion annually. The air traveler pays but one third of the cost of air travel. On the other hand, the total amount of government assistance to Amtrak from Fiscal Year 1971 through 1978 has amounted to approximately $2.5 billion.[6] This is just a drop in the bucket compared to what has been handed out to the non-rail transportation interests.

Another interesting fact is that the railroad industry received about $200 million in government assistance between 1920 and 1971, but the figure is greatly misleading. It is also well known that the railroads received substantial land grants from the government during the 1800's. In return for the grants, the railroads were required to haul government freight and passenger traffic (not just the Military, but other organizations as well, such as the Tennessee Valley Authority) at reduced rates. And here is the "kicker." The total amount of the deductions amounted to $580 million through June 30, 1943.[7] It is not known what the amount was after that date. Congress relieved the railroads from further obligations of rate reductions on October 1, 1946. It should be noted that this figure is several times the value of the land grants at the time they were made, and also exceeding the sums derived by the railroads from the grants.

The point is brought out here because the railroads have paid through the nose for any subsidies that they may have secured. It indeed put the railroad industry on a shakey footing, and the rail passenger service suffered most of all.

The third argument is that the bus companies pay taxes as any private enterprise. True, but only half the story. Amtrak's annual tax bill is twice that of the entire bus industry.[8] In reality, neither the bus, the trucking industry, nor the air industry pay their true portion of the usage of the government provided transport system, highway or air. This has worked to the detriment of the railroad industry and the U.S. as a whole.

Admittedly subsidies are a controversial subject. Many can argue that subsidies are justified on the grounds of social, political, national defense and other non-economic benefits. However the fact remains that highway and air line operators, both public and private, are not paying their fair share of facility usage and therefore cannot attack Amtrak's financial support in view of their own support over several decades.

In reality, instead of thinking of profit and loss during this period of transportation crisis, one should be thinking of comparative economics. According to Garth Campbell, Vice President of Via Rail Canada, comparative economics has to do with the cost of providing a given service. The Japanese had the problem of what to do about the transportation between Tokyo and Osaka. Campbell commented that they had three basic options: new highways, new airports and the high speed rail line. (The latter was eventually built and is successfully operating— at a profit one might add.) According to Campbell, the railroad was the least attractive and had the least amount of supporters. *However, when the Japanese put all the figures down on paper, the railroad was by far the most economic use of land, of energy and just basic everyday operating costs.*[9]   Therefore the problem can be summed up as one of ignoring the cost of service. The same is true of the airlines. For example, if the U.S. were to remove its subsidies to the airlines, a round trip ticket between the west and east coast would cost over one thousand dollars.[10] The nation is not looking at transportation costs realistically at all.

The highways in the U.S. were in relatively good shape until about 1970. However, since then the picture has been changing rapidly. As of 1978, hundreds of thousands of miles of highways and more than 100,000 bridges need major overhaul or replacement. The cost of upkeep and renovation is estimated to be over $329 billion over the next ten years.[11]

It appears to this writer that former Transportation Secretary Brock Adams was not particularly friendly toward the railroad industry or Amtrak. One wonders why some of the government leaders cannot realize that by reshaping our thinking and utilizing the railroad industry more effectively, the country could save billions of dollars. In turn, the airlines, trucking and bus industry would be better utilized for what they are best suited. The country's economic health would improve substantially. With fewer automobiles, there would be fewer accidents, fewer highway deaths, and far less property damage costs due to accidents. And incidently, highway accidents and deaths are a very significant, but hidden, cost of highway transportation.

Admittedly, the automotive manufacturers would not be happy with the prospects of fewer sales. However, they could adjust and the displaced workers could switch to the public transportation industry. Further, Ford and Chrysler could re-tool to build railroad cars and locomotives. General Motors is already in the locomotive business. In addition, with less usage of the automobile, more buses would be required. The plants could be re-tooled to build buses and it is not unlikely that the automobile companies might be more profitable than ever. Consequently, the auto industry need not suffer, and in fact, the country will always need the automobile.

It is because of all of these problems that the passenger train must be considered seriously. Louis Harris and Associates found that sixty per cent of Americans want the federal government to spend more money on faster and more comfortable trains; and believe that providing faster and more comfortable trains is very important.[12] Apparently, the American people are willing to look at the problem realistically.

The energy crisis also plays a part in the need for the passenger train. Energy usage, discussed earlier in this chapter, would be improved substantially by the creation of a balanced transportation system in North America.

The energy crisis is indeed most interesting. It sometimes appears that the general public does

RELATIVE FUEL EFFICIENCY
Amtrak Amfleet Trains vs. the Intercity Motorbus
A comparison at 50 mph

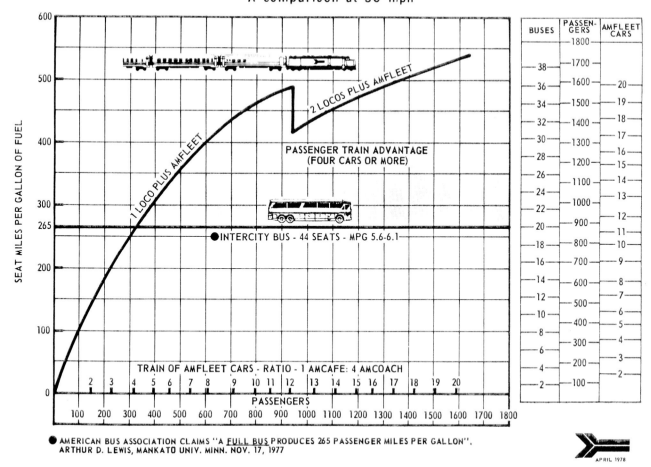

● AMERICAN BUS ASSOCIATION CLAIMS "A <u>FULL BUS</u> PRODUCES 265 PASSENGER MILES PER GALLON".
ARTHUR D. LEWIS, MANKATO UNIV. MINN. NOV. 17, 1977

APRIL 1978

This particular graph illustrates the fuel efficiencies of the Amfleet train versus the Intercity bus at a speed of 50 miles per hour. (Amtrak)

not realize that a crisis exists. One frequently hears comments that there is plenty of oil and that oil companies are "ripping off" the public. Let's assume for a moment that this is true. Does this mean that the same will be true 10 years from now? 20 years from now? Most likely not because there is a finite supply of oil and when it's gone it's gone! This generation has a responsibility to future generations and cannot act as though the world is going to end in the next fifty years and use everything up. Coal can be used to produce gas, gasoline and electric power and other products until the time comes when direct sun power can be stored and used efficiently. One might say the world has about 300 years to develop this power. Trains can be powered by coal either directly (steam) or through electric transmission, thereby leaving the precious oil for home heating and other more important crucial uses, instead of for automobiles. Cutting auto mileage by 10 to 20% over the next five years will improve our oil reserves, whatever they might be. The oil can't last forever, and the country has too much of a dependency on the Middle East. When the next oil embargo comes, and it will come, the U.S. is going to be in serious trouble. However, Americans have had a tradition of not doing anything until there is crisis. One could ask, why change now? The answer to that is, why wait until it is too late?

The need for the passenger train and more importantly the need for a National Transportation Policy clearly does exist. However, until all concerned are willing to look at the situation realistically, including the railroads themselves, the passenger train and Amtrak as a controversial subject is going to be around for awhile.

Chapter 2
History and Development
of Amtrak

The history and development of the National Railroad Passenger Corporation is, perhaps, the most unusual chapter in North American railroading since the 1830's. The fact that a segment of the USA's transportation system has been nationalized is not so unusual in terms of world history. Indeed, with the exception of Canada, virtually all transportation organizations all over the world are run by their respective governments. (The government owned Canadian National Railways are not run by the government. CN is a crown corporation and politics are out. This is one reason why CN is profitable and other nationalized railways are not. The reason why CN often shows an overall loss is the interest payments on the past debts of the former railways, which were not cancelled as has been the case with other government takeovers throughout the world.) What is so unusual is that the nationalization of the railroad passenger service is the first step, not toward nationalization of the entire railroad industry, but hopefully toward the development of a balanced transportation industry throughout the USA. Further, it marks for the first time that rail passenger transportation has received any type of support from the U.S. Government in contrast to the decades of its financial and other types of support to non-rail modes of transport to freight as well as passenger. This has brought about almost a total collapse of the nation's railroad system.

In COACH TRAINS & TRAVEL, this author explored the decline in rail patronage from 1929 when the nation's railroads carried 77% of the intercity passenger traffic on some 20,000 trains. This number decreased to about 9,000 trains in 1950 with the rail share of the pie amounting to less than ½ of the total traffic. Bus traffic, on the other hand, increased to over 37% with air over 14%. By 1970, the rail share was just over 7% with but 450 trains still in service, and well over 75% of those trains earmarked by the companies for discontinuance. About 100 petitions had already been made, and it was quite apparent that by 1976 there would be only a handful of trains left. It is interesting to note that the slice of air traffic had grown to 73% while the bus industry lost ground and held on to barely 16% of the intercity public transportation traffic. What was actually happening, was that the three major modes were dividing up about 12% of the total intercity traffic, with the automobile handling nearly 88% of all intercity transportation in 1971. The result: a serious imbalance in the nation's transportation network.

Now the United States could live with such an imbalance if the population did not continue to grow, if the world had an unlimited supply of petroleum (eventually it has to run out) and if the automobile did not create so many additional problems, such as air and noise pollution, not to mention the annual death and property damage rates. Not only are the highways overcrowded, but the air routes are too. Both modes of transport have demanded excessive land use and dislocation of people during the past decade, and the situation in the late 1960's indicated that it would continue to get worse. Consequently, it became apparent that the USA could not live with the imbalance in its transportation system. Something had to be done, and the railway system is the ONLY system capable of handling people (and large numbers of them) safely, economically and with all weather dependability.

Should there be any doubt as to the validity of that statement, one should ride a Metroliner anytime and observe the traffic on parallel expressways. Ride it again during bad weather and note the worsening of the situation. Or perhaps better still drive and watch the Metroliners and other streamliners streaking by in rain or shine, snow or sleet. The point is that the highway system cannot continue the strangulation of our central cities and our air systems have reached, or will soon reach, their capacity. The only solution to the problem is to redevelop our rail passenger system which should not have been allowed to deteriorate in the first place.

Consequently, the USA has gone through and still is in a period of dark ages of public transportation.

The problem has been recognized by congress and other leaders throughout the USA, and on October 30, 1970, President Nixon signed the Rail Passenger Service Act, which authorized the National Railroad Passenger Corporation to manage the basic national rail network and be responsible for the operation of all intercity passenger trains under contracts with the railroads.

The corporation received an initial federal grant of $40 million in cash, $100 million in loans guaranteed by the Federal government, and approximately $197 million in entry fee payments from the railroads, payable in monthly installments over a three year period. That funding, and other types have been expanded since then and it has enabled Amtrak to solve its motive power equipment problems. For example, in 1974, Amtrak was granted authority to borrow as much as $500 million for capital improvements in new rolling stock and facilities.

May 1, 1971 will long be remembered in the railroad industry as Amtrak day, for on that day the new corporation assumed the responsibility of managaing the intercity passenger service between twenty-one city pair end points designated by Transportation Secretary Volpe on January 28, 1971. Virtually all railroads except for freight lines, such as the Frisco and the Soo Line signed contracts with Amtrak. A number of lines did elect not to join, such as Southern, Rock Island, Rio Grande, Chicago South Shore & South Bend, Georgia, Reading and Central of New Jersey. Still other roads joined but originally did not operate Amtrak services such as Chicago & North Western. Some of the non-member roads as of 1979 still operate passenger service.

Since the initial announcement of route selections on March 22, 1971, Amtrak has continuously examined and re-evaluated the system to determine if additional service is needed on existing routes, or if other adjustments are necessary. Consequently, the Corporation has made many changes since May 1, 1971. For example, train service via the former New York Central between Chicago and New York was added shortly after start up, and later discontinued. Then in late 1975, the train service was resumed on a Chicago-Boston-New York run. Amtrak has some freedom to conduct such changes, which unfortunately the ICC did not allow the railroad industry to do. Indeed, many railroad managers have conceded that if the ICC had allowed the railroads to operate the present Amtrack service, they would have been far less willing to give the service up. The Rail Passenger Service Act of 1970 provides Amtrak with this freedom.

Another provision under this act is for the participation by states or regional agencies in service not included in the basic network. Such an agency can petition the Corporation to provide service so long as it is prepared to pay half of the fully allocated loss incurred in operating the service. The Illinois Zephyr between Chicago and Quincy and the Blue Water between Chicago and Port Huron are two examples of this type of service.

The original act did not provide for international train service. Congress, however, authorized such service on June 22, 1972 and Amtrak now operates trains to Vancouver and Montreal.

After the Board of Incorporaters had announced the basic route selections, Amtrak began the task of managing the nation's intercity passenger trains on that first day of May in 1971. Its aim was and is to reverse the downward trends of ridership and revenue and curtail uneconomic service. It also meant that for the first time in history, a unified, centrally managed nationwide complete railroad passenger network was formed— able to provide uniform and rising standards of service for all United States citizens. (The Pullman Company was also a nationwide passenger operation, but covered primarily sleeping car service and very little coach service.)

It took time to really get started. Changes were made immediately with the original routes, such as the addition of a Minneapolis-Spokane via Butte run on June 14, 1971. Amtrak also began the task of advertising rail service, which had been done very little by the railroad industry up to this point. Not only were the newspapers, radio and TV put to use, but a month long tour of the Turbo began on August 11, 1971. The train toured the entire country and introduced a new travel concept to Americans. The tour of the Turbo whet the appetite of many Americans for train travel and the benefits from that tour are still being realized several years later.

November, 1971 marked a complete change in many of the operating procedures. In order to avoid confusion with the computerized reservation system, all duplicate train numbers had to be changed and many of the trains received new names. A new employee training program also began that month.

In early 1972, Amtrak made attempts to bring about a co-ordinated transportation system by setting up forty tour packages to key tourist areas, with many of them on a joint basis with Greyhound Bus Lines.

Late 1972 brought some new developments that began to show that Amtrak had the potential to succeed. The Louis Harris national opinion survey reported that a majority of Americans favored improvements in rail passenger service, and that there was indeed a demand for it. The third quarter revenues in 1972 were up 13.2% over the same period in 1971 and seemed to bear out the Harris poll.

The result: the first new equipment was ordered

TABLE 5 — PHILADELPHIA - HARRISBURG (Penn Central) (E.T.)

Westbound

	Miles	601 Ex. Sat. and Sun.	603 Ex. Sun.	25 Daily	605 Ex. Sat. and Sun.	607 Daily	633 Daily	609 Ex. Sat. and Sun.	611 Ex. Sat. and Sun.	617 Sat. and Sun. only	613 Ex. Sat. and Sun.	49 Daily	615 Ex. Sat.
				The Duquesne								*Broadway Limited*	
PHILADELPHIA [LEAVE]		A M	A M	A M 9 01	A M	A M	A M	P M	P M	P M	P M	P M 6 21	P M
North Philadelphia▲	0	5 41	5 58		10 25	12 42	2 05	3 25	5 28	5 55	6 20		9 50
Penn Center		5 45			10 28	12 45	2 08	3 28	5 31	5 58	6 23		9 53
Penn Central Station (30th Street)		5 48											
Ardmore	9	6 21	8 00	9 23	10 51	1 07	2 30	3 50		6 20	6 45	6 55	10 15
Bryn Mawr	10	6 34	8 03			1 20	2 42	4 04	6 03		6 47		10 17
Paoli	20	6 47	8 13		10 57	1 26	2 48	4 09	6 08		6 59	7 05	10 24
Malvern	28	6 53	8 27	9 39	11 03				6 13		7 05		10 29
Whitford	30												
Downingtown▲	33	7 00	8 39	9 46	11 09	1 35		4 37	6 19		7 10	7 10	10 35
Parkesburg▲	39	d7 04	8 45										
Coatesville	44		8 49		11 22	1 52		4 53	6 45		7 19		
Lancaster	68	7 07	9 11		11 35	2 14		5 10			7 32	7 40	11 01
Mount Joy▲	79	7 19	9 27							7 02			11 17
Elizabethtown▲	86	7 26					3 14		7 02				
Middletown▲	94	7 33	9 38			2 22	3 47		7 19	7 21	7 48		
HARRISBURG [ARRIVE]	103	7 45	9 45	10 25	12 07	2 25		5 55	7 38		8 05	8 25	11 34

Will not run May 31, July 5 or September 6.
Also runs May 31, July 5 and September 6.

TABLE 5 — HARRISBURG - PHILADELPHIA

Eastbound

	600 Ex. Sat. and Sun.	48 Daily	602 Ex. Sun.	604 Daily	606 Daily	608 Ex. Sun.	618 Daily	610 Daily	612 Sat. and Sun.	16 Daily	614 Daily
		Broadway Limited								*The Duquesne*	
HARRISBURG [LEAVE]	A M 5 41	A M 6 25	A M 6 50	A M 8 00	A M 10 05	P M 12 35	P M 3 00	P M 4 25	P M 5 25	P M 6 05	P M 7 55
Middletown▲	5 58		6 59	8 16				4 41	5 40		
Elizabethtown▲	6 15		7 22	8 33	10 37	1 07	3 33	4 58	5 47	6 38	8 27
Mount Joy▲	6 19		d7 43				3 59		5 54		
Lancaster	6 45	7 01	7 49	8 49	11 03	1 33	4 05	5 30	6 07	6 50	8 53
Coatesville	6 48		7 55	9 05	11 12	1 39	4 17	5 42	6 32		8 59
Parkesburg▲	6 53		7 58								
Downingtown▲	7 00	d7 48	d8 06	9 19	11 22	1 51	4 37	5 55	6 38	7 10	9 11
Whitford	7 04		8 09						6 45		
Malvern											
Paoli	7 29		8 34	9 44	11 50	2 18	4 41	6 06	7 14	7 29	9 34
Bryn Mawr	7 33	8 21	8 38	9 48	11 54	2 22	4 45	6 10	7 18	7 56	9 38
Ardmore											
PHILADELPHIA											
Penn Central Station (30th Street)											
Penn Center▲											
North Philadelphia▲	A M	A M	A M	A M	A M	P M	P M	P M	P M	P M	P M

Trains not listed carry coaches only.
No baggage service between Philadelphia and Harrisburg.

EQUIPMENT

WESTBOUND

Train No. 25 — The Duquesne
- Snack Bar Coach—Hot-Cold Food and Beverages—Philadelphia-Harrisburg
- Reclining Seat Coaches....................Between all points

Train No. 49 — Broadway Limited
- Lounge Buffet..................................Philadelphia-Harrisburg
- Dining Car.......................................Philadelphia-Harrisburg
- Reclining Seat Coaches (*All Seats Reserved*)...Philadelphia-Harrisburg
- Coach Attendant Service)..Philadelphia-Harrisburg

EASTBOUND

Train No. 16 — The Duquesne
- Snack Bar Coach—Hot-Cold Food and Beverages—Harrisburg-Philadelphia
- Reclining Seat Coaches....................Between all points

Train No. 48 — Broadway Limited
- Lounge Buffet..................................Harrisburg-Philadelphia
- Dining Car.......................................Harrisburg-Philadelphia
- Reclining Seat Coaches (*All Seats Reserved*)...Harrisburg-Philadelphia
- Coach Attendant Service).Harrisburg-Philadelphia

EXPLANATION OF SIGNS

c Stops only to receive passengers.
d Stops only to discharge passengers.
f Stops only on signal or notice to agent or conductor to receive or discharge passengers.
x Stops Monday thru Friday except holidays.
ç Stops Saturday, Sunday and holidays only.
E Receives passengers for points west of Paoli.
▲No facilities for handling baggage at this station. Baggage should be checked to or from nearest station where facilities are available.
(*E.T.*)—Eastern time.

TABLE 6 — NEW YORK - ALBANY - BUFFALO (VIA ALBANY-SYRACUSE) (Penn Central) (E.T.)

Northbound

	New York (Grand Central) Leave	Croton-Harmon	Pough-keepsie	Rhinecliff	Hudson	Albany-Rensse-laer Arrive	Colonie-Schene-ctady	Utica	Syracuse	Rochester	Batavia	Buffalo Arrive
No. ◆71—Daily	8 30 A M	9 22 A M	10 00 A M		10 35 A M	11 10 A M	11 30 A M	12 45	1 40 P M	2 50 P M	3 25	4 00 P M
No. ◆81—Daily	10 30 A M	11 22 A M	12 00 Noon	12 15 P M	12 35	1 10 P M		4 45	5 40 P M	6 50		8 00 P M
No. ◆73—Daily	12 30 P M	1 22 P M	2 00 P M	2 15	3 10	3 30 P M						
No. ◆83—Daily	2 30 P M	3 22	4 00	4 15	4 35	5 10						
No. ◆75—Daily	4 30 P M	5 22	6 00	6 15	6 35	7 10 P M	7 30	8 45	9 40 P M	10 50		12 00 Night
No. ◆61—Daily	6 30 P M	7 22	8 00	8 15	8 35	9 10						
No. ◆85—Daily	8 30 P M	9 22 P M	10 00 P M	10 15	10 35	11 10 P M						

TABLE 6 — BUFFALO - ALBANY - NEW YORK (VIA SYRACUSE - ALBANY)

Southbound

	Buffalo Leave	Batavia	Rochester	Syracuse	Utica	Colonie-Schene-ctady	Albany-Rensse-laer Leave	Hudson	Rhinecliff	Pough-keepsie	Croton-Harmon	New York (Grand Central) Arrive
No. ◆62—Daily	6 30 A M		7 30 A M	8 50 A M	9 30 A M		10 45 A M					2 00 P M
No. ◆80—Daily							11 20 A M					
No. ◆72—Daily	10 30 A M		11 30	12 50 P M	1 30 P M	1 20	2 45 P M	1 45	2 05	2 20	3 05	4 00 P M
No. ◆82—Daily						3 20						
No. ◆84—Daily						5 20	5 20 P M	5 45	6 05	6 20	7 05	8 00 P M
No. ◆74—Daily	2 30 P M		3 30	4 50	5 30	7 20	6 45 P M	7 20				10 00 P M

EQUIPMENT

Train Nos. 73 and 75
- Coaches....................New York-Buffalo
- Snack Bar Coach.........New York-Albany

Train Nos. 61 and 62
- Coaches....................New York-Albany
- Snack Bar Coach.........New York-Albany

Train Nos. 70 and 72
- Coaches....................New York-Buffalo
- Snack Bar Coach.........New York-Buffalo

Train Nos. 71 and 74
- Coaches....................New York-Buffalo
- Snack Bar Coach.........New York-Buffalo
- Baggage Car...............New York-Buffalo

TABLE 7 — NEW YORK - PITTSBURGH - CHICAGO (Penn Central)

No. 49 Daily	No. ◆25 Daily	Miles		No. 48 Daily	No. ◆16 Daily
4 55 P M	7 35 A M	0	lve.NEW YORK (R.T.)arr. (Pennsylvania Station)	9 50 A M	9 25 P M
5 11 P M	7 51 A M	10	Newark	9 34 A M	9 09 P M
5 55	8 45 A M	58	Trenton	8 48	8 24 P M
6 21	9 01 A M	85	North Philadelphia	d7 48	7 29
6 55 P M	9 48 A M	111	Paoli	7 25	7 10 P M
7 40 P M	9 48 A M	130	Coatesville	7 01 A M	6 38 P M
8 35	10 25 A M	159	Lancaster	6 25 A M	6 10
	11 11 P M	194	Harrisburg		5 50 P M
	12 21 P M	255	Lewistown		4 40
	12 56 P M	291	Huntingdon		3 59 P M
11 11 P M	1 52 P M	325	Altoona	3 43 A M	3 14
12 09 A M	2 51 P M	362	Johnstown		2 07 P M
1 42 A M	3 41 P M	399	Latrobe		1 30
	4 50 P M	439	arr.Pittsburgh..lve. (Penn Central Station)	1 16 A M	12 30 P M
		541	lve.Pittsburgh..arr. Canton	f10 10 P M	
fg 51 A M		628	Crestline	9 31 P M	
5 34 A M		700	Lima	8 20	
7 35 A M		759	Ft. Wayne (E.T.)	7 23 P M	
8 25 A M		882	Gary (C.T.)	4 33	
9 00 A M		907	arr. CHICAGO (C.T.)lve. (Union Station)	4 00 P M	

EQUIPMENT

Train Nos. 16 and 25—Duquesne
- Coach................................New York-Pittsburgh
- Snack Bar Coach................New York-Pittsburgh

Train Nos. 48 and 49—Broadway Limited
- Coaches...............................New York-Chicago
- Diner.....................................New York-Chicago
- Lounge-Coach Bar..................New York-Chicago
- Sleeper Coach—Single Bedrooms, Double Bedrooms....New York-Chicago
- Sleepers—Roomettes, Double Bedrooms..New York-Chicago

EXPLANATION OF SIGNS

✓ Stops only on signal or notice to agent or conductor to receive or discharge passengers.
◆ No baggage service on this train.
▲ No facilities for handling baggage at this station. Baggage should be checked to or from nearest station where facilities are handled.
(*C.T.*)—Central time.
(*E.T.*)—Eastern time.

Example of early Amtrak time table utilizing original railroad train numbers. (May 1, 1971)

(Turboliners) and there was cause for optimism as Amtrak celebrated its 2nd anniversary with ceremonies in both Washington and Chicago on May 1, 1973. A variety of newly refurbished equipment was on display in both cities for the event and Amtrak President Roger Lewis noted that the yearly decline in train ridership that continued for decades had been reversed and started on the upgrade. It was time to consider placing an order for a vast amount of new train equipment.

In mid-1973, Amtrak asked American industry to design a new generation of rail passenger cars and to incorporate the best available transportation technology into the design. It finally appeared that the dark ages of passenger car design and construction were finally coming to an end. Amtrak President Roger Lewis stated that the new Amtrak standard would combine maximum saleable space with the best attainable ride quality at speeds up to 120 miles per hour on conventional track. In addition, he said, Amtrak wanted a car that could be flexible enough so that interiors could be changed easily to meet changing markets.

A total of 13 U.S. manufacturing and industrial design firms were contacted. These included the traditional railroad car manufacturers (such as Budd and Pullman), large diversified manufacturers, industrial design firms and four aerospace com-

INTERCITY RAILROAD
National Railroad
PASSENGER ROUTES
Passenger Corporation

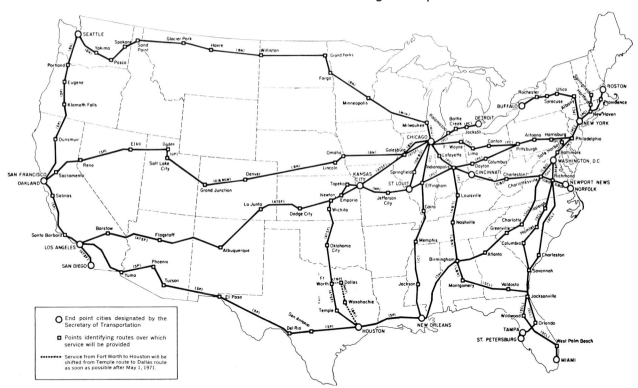

○ End point cities designated by the Secretary of Transportation

▫ Points identifying routes over which service will be provided

▪▪▪▪▪▪▪▪ Service from Fort Worth to Houston will be shifted from Temple route to Dallas route as soon as possible after May 1, 1971.

This is the first Amtrak map showing the routes of the various trains as they were supposed to be on May 1, 1971. However, the map was soon incorrect — even for the first day — because the Rio Grande elected not to join and the Chicago-San Francisco train was re-routed over the Union Pacific between Denver and Ogden, Utah. Another difference was the inclusion of the Southern Railway between Washington, D.C. and New Orleans. The Southern Railway did not elect to join Amtrak until February 1, 1979. (Amtrak, May 1, 1971 time table)

INTERCITY RAIL PASSENGER ROUTES
National Railroad Passenger Corporation

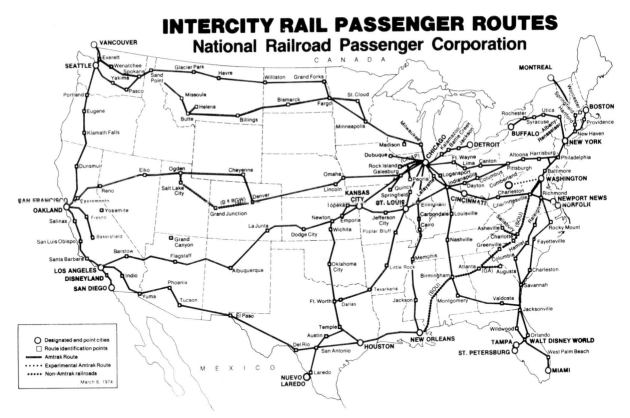

About three years later, there were a number of differences on the map as compared to May 1, 1971. New routes, such as the Montrealer and the North Coast, were giving the map a much more healthy look. (Amtrak, March 6, 1974)

panies. At that time, Lewis said that a successful design would be used by Amtrak in taking bids for an initial order of at least 100 new passenger cars that could be used on all Amtrak routes. (This later turned into the large Amfleet orders to the Budd Company.) The first step had been taken to solve the critical passenger car equipment problem.

Another problem of great magnitude was the reservation system. In Chicago, for example, there were six different numbers to call depending on which railroad had formerly operated the particular train the passenger wished to take. Amtrak had inherited 13 different manual systems that were designed in the 1930's. The first step was to set up an interim "make do" system. Then plans were made for a modern nationwide computerized system designed to make buying a train ticket as easy as dialing the phone.

While the airlines had developed modern and efficient reservation techniques, there was not a system in the world that could serve Amtrak's more compli-

cated requirements. Amtrak's multiplicity of stops, fares and accommodations required a totally new system if rail passengers were to be served efficiently and quickly. Amtrak found it necessary to have schedule and fare information for over 12,500 origin-destination cities with up to 30 different fares available between cities for 13 different accommodations plus a variety of special fares. This adds up to over 360,000 different fare possiblities. All these factors were responsible for the development of the Advanced Reservation and Ticketing System, known as ARTS.

The ARTS system revolves around two Control Data 3500 computers located at Amtrak headquarters in Washington, D.C. Five centralized reservation offices at Bensalem, Pa.; Jacksonville, Florida, New York City, Chicago and Los Angeles are also tied into the computer.

The first of these centers, Bensalem, went into operation April 15, 1973 serving the Northeast from Virginia to Canada. The first day of operations the agents handled 3,000 calls and did not lose a single caller. Each phone was answered within an average of six seconds, compared to the previous system when calls were frequently not answered at all. Bensalem handles as many as 16,000 calls a day and

18

INTERCITY RAIL PASSENGER ROUTES
National Railroad Passenger Corporation

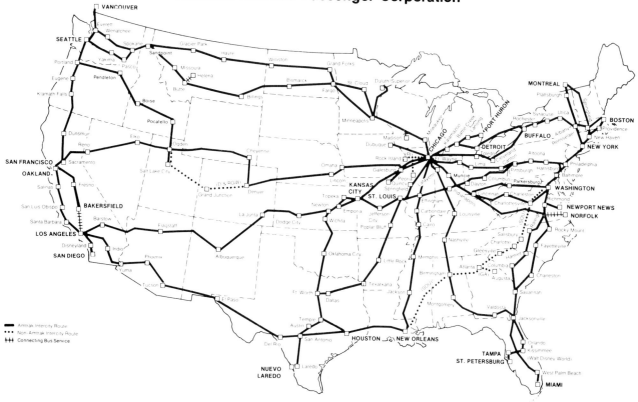

The **mid-1977 map** reflected not only the railroad lines, but also the connecting bus routes, such as between Bakersfield and Los Angeles. Except for the Southern Railway, which became a heavy black line in early 1979, the 1977 map reflected the basic Amtrak train services through most of 1979. (Amtrak, June, 1977)

the percentage handled seldom falls below 95% and frequently hovers at the 99 to 100% mark.

When a caller makes a toll-free call to inquire about reservations, the call is answered by an agent at one of the five centers. While the caller waits, the agent types the request into a visual display terminal, which looks much like a television screen. The information is transmitted via telephone lines to the computers. With the speed of light, the computers scan their millions of memory cells, find the right one, and send the information back to the agent where it appears on the console screen. The computer can make the reservation if that is what the passenger wishes, or if he requires information only, the computer feeds back information on all trains for a particular destination on a particular date including the necessary fare information. If a reservation is made the computer can automatically send an advisory report to the depot where the ticket will be picked up.

The various centers are equipped with sophisticated monitoring systems. A flashing digital box reads out exactly what is going on at the center at

all times. It shows how many agents are on duty, how many incoming calls are waiting, how long the oldest call has been waiting, how many agents are in conversation with customers, how many customers are on hold while the agent seeks additional information from another source by phone and how many agents are making call backs or working on follow-up duties. In addition, calls can be switched from a heavy workload area to another center which is less busy. ARTS represents an initial $7 million investment for Amtrak and has revolutionized reseration procedures.

By the time Amtrak was three years old on May 1, 1974, things were really moving optimistically. Nearly 1,400 of the passenger cars purchased from the railroads had undergone heavy overhaul and refurbishment. The bulk of the 150 new 3,000 horse-

In the past far too many ticket offices were dingy and poorly lit. Not very inviting for prospective train travelers. Amtrak has spruced up, rebuilt and modernized many offices with clean, well lit ticket windows complete (hopefully) with a smiling, courteous and knowledgeable ticket agent. The first step for the rail traveler. (Amtrak)

power diesel locomotive order was in service before the end of that summer along with 50 older locomotives which were rebuilt. Also on order were 57 non-powered Metroliner type coaches (now known as Amfleet cars) and 26 electric locomotives. The reservation problems had been solved, and most of the employees whom passengers met in stations, on the trains or on the phone worked for Amtrak. These were and are the service employees: clerks, waiters, car attendants, train directors, passenger service representatives and red caps. Nearly all were dressed in the now familiar red Amtrak jacket. Engineers, conductors and brakemen still work for the railroads. The number of Amtrak employees at the end of April, 1974 stood at 8,000. Patronage in 1974 was at various times running nearly 40% over the previous year, mostly because of a gasoline fuel crisis.

Amtrak was adding new routes, such as Oakland-Bakersfield, St. Louis and Laredo, Texas and new trains on regular routes, such as the Expo '74 between Seattle and Spokane. The total passenger carrying capacity of Amtrak during the summer of 1974 was almost double what it was during the summer of 1971. Yes, things were definitely looking up; but there were still problems, many of them to be sure.

Besides equipment problems, Amtrak announced AUTO-TRAK. Auto-Trak was to be an auto ferry system, similar to Auto Train, between the midwest and Florida. Passengers, it was reported, would be able to load their automobiles on an Amtrak train at Indianapolis and reclaim them at Poinciana, Florida. Experimental runs were conducted, but service was not implemented because Auto-Train wanted to begin service on a similar route.

Other problems were caused by the rampant inflation. Increased costs went up faster than revenues, and it necessitated a selective fare adjustment in November, 1973 and an across-the-board 5% increase in April, 1974. A 20% summer peak season surcharge was added to Amtrak western trains between June 9 and September 7, 1974.

The year 1974's substantial increases in passenger traffic brought even more problems to Amtrak. Many trains during the spring were running with standing room only, and on May 19th, Amtrak began requiring reservations for all coach seats on long distance trains. The following trains went on an "All-Reserved" basis:

> San Francisco Zephyr
> Empire Builder
> North Coast Hiawatha
> Lone Star
> Inter-American
> National Limited
> James Whitcomb Riley
> Panama Limited
> Montrealer
> Night Owl

At the time, there were already several "All Reserved" trains in operation, such as the Broadway Limited, the Coast Starlight and the Sunset Limited. The Florida trains were also on an All Reserved status, even though some of those trains operated only on a seasonal basis.

The increases in business prompted Amtrak to announce on June 6, 1974 that orders for 200 passenger cars (the Amfleet) and six high speed five car turbine trains were placed with the Budd Company and a French railroad equipment builder. This brought the total of Amfleet cars to 257 plus the 30 cars in the six five car sets. When delivered, the new equipment would add about 40% to Amtrak's passenger carrying capacity, or in other words, 22,816 new seats added to the 57,000 in service in 1974. At the same time 25 additional diesel locomotives were ordered primarily to power the forthcoming Amfleet. Plans were made in 1974 to use the Amfleet primarily on routes along the eastern seaboard, while the new turbine trains would be used on routes radiating out of Chicago, and maintained at Amtrak's New Brighton Park maintenance facility.

All of the new cars ordered in mid-1974, including the six turbine trains, were to be fitted with advanced type suspension systems to improve ride quality as well as all-electric air conditioning and heating systems. It was expected that all 257 Amfleet cars would be delivered by May, 1976. The total price tag for the additional 200 cars was $81 million.

Of the six Turboliners, Amtrak already had two of the trains in service between Chicago and St. Louis since October, 1973. The trains compiled a 99% reliability record for the first four months of 1974. The trains were leased from ANF-Frangeco of Crespin, France, which was also building 41 of the same train sets for the French National Railways. The additional four French made Turboliners were shipped to Amtrak during late 1974 and early 1975 and placed in service on the St. Louis, Detroit, Milwaukee and Port Huron routes. (Amfleet eventually replaced the Turboliners on the St. Louis routes.) The total cost of the 308 seat turbine trains, including shipping to the United States, import duty, initial spare parts and equipment added by Amtrak after arrival was around $18 million. The lease payments were credited toward the purchase price.

Mid-1974 brought additional locomotive orders. On June 24, Amtrak ordered 25 more 3,000 horsepower diesel locomotives. The new locomotives were built by General Electric and delivery took place during 1975. This brought the total of new diesel locomotives purchased by Amtrak to 175, with 150 being purchased from Electro-Motive Division of General Motors. The new General Electric engines were designed to power electric heating, air conditioning and other auxiliary equipment in the 257 Amfleet cars ordered from the Budd Company.

In September, 1974, a five year financial plan for substantial new passenger car and locomotive purchases, assumption of repair and maintenance functions from the railroads and a major track improvement program was sent to the Congress and the Department of Transportation.

Amtrak President Roger Lewis commented that the plan (approved by Amtrak's Board of Directors) would lead to funding the company's operating plan through fiscal year 1976 and capital program through fiscal year 1979. He further commented that the plan was designed to carry out Amtrak's mandate from Congress that "modern, efficient, intercity rail passenger service is a necessary part of a balanced transportation system" and that "Continuance and improvement of such service is clearly in the public interest."

According to the Amtrak News Release dated Monday, September 9, 1974, President Lewis stated, "Our three years of operations have demonstrated that a real demand for rail passenger service exists, and is certain to grow, especially when

Even small town depots have been repainted and given new signs, such as Wisconsin Dells, Wisconsin on the double track Milwaukee Road main line. (Patrick C. Dorin)

To assist ticket agents is a computer system. Each agent, either at a major depot or telephone contact, has access to a terminal which provides up to date information concerning available space on board Amtrak System trains. The terminals are easy to operate, almost as simple as typing on a typewriter. In 1979 the system is working quite well and has made rail travel much easier. (Amtrak)

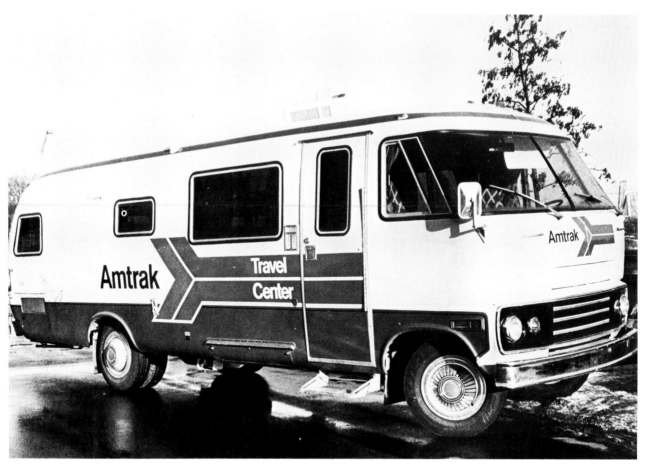

Amtrak sales personnel have taken to the highways with a specially outfitted 27 foot-long motor home designed to bring the message of what train travel is to thousands of travel agents across the U.S.A. The travel center shows train interiors, a slide show and a dining car set up, and stocks all the literature and forms needed to help agents sell rail travel. (Amtrak)

viewed in context with the nation's continuing energy supply problems. A program of this magnitude is necessary to revitalize intercity train service."

The capital program called for an immediate purchase of 235 double deck long distance cars and 200 additional Amfleet cars as well as 25 electric locomotives at an estimated cost of $263 million. These were in addition to the 257 Amfleet cars and the 201 diesel and electric locomotives previously ordered.

The plan also contemplated a modest expansion of route structure as provided in the Amtrak Act, and assumed there would be long distance and short haul, state subsidized routes added during each of the five years from 1974 through 1979.

In October, 1974, the Southern Railway and Amtrak signed an agreement under which Amtrak's nationwide toll free computerized reservation and information system, ARTS, began handling Southern's reservations and information. Information about all Southern's trains was included along with Amtrak services in the ARTS computers, and ticketing for Southern trains and Amtrak trains and connections between the two were possible. Southern paid Amtrak for the cost of the computer services plus all supplied equipment installed on Southern. Southern joined Amtrak on February 1, 1979.

By October, 1974, the complete Automatic Reservation and Ticketing System was totally installed with the central computer system located in Washington with the five regional reservation and information center handling about 65,000 calls per day.

1974 was a record year for Amtrak. During the summer Amtrak carried more passengers more miles than in any previous summer despite having fewer seats available on most key routes. Amtrak carried 4,351,234 passengers during the three summer months of 1974 as compared to 3,892,552 the

When Amtrak acquired the former Penn Central coach yards, Chicago, they were in such run-down condition that portions of the facility were totally unusable without substantial upgrading. By 1978, the yard was about half way through the renovation project with these modern concrete ramps between tracks providing easy access to all equipment. Equipment for several trains can be seen in this photo. Some of the Amfleet equipment is being readied for the Black Hawk, State House, Panama Limited, Illini and the Illinois Zephyr, while the standard streamlined equipment on the right is for the Floridian (with domes), the Broadway and Lake Shore Limiteds. With the cleaner surroundings and the new and rebuilt equipment, activity at the 12th Street coach yards is just as exciting as ever. (Amtrak)

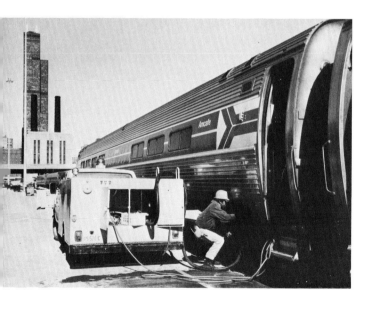

The new concrete ramps at 12th Street permit the use of mobile units designed to service both the Amfleet and the Superliners. (Amtrak)

summer before. The system wide increase was 11%. At the same time, revenue passenger miles increased 20% in June, 7% in July and 3% in August over comparable 1973 figures. The available seat miles in 1974 were less by 4% in July and 10% in August than in 1973. The reduction was caused by an increasing number of cars needing repairs because of age, and the number of cars had to be spread over more routes and expanded service. It was a tough period of time, but Amtrak was able to handle the influx of traffic. Many Amtrak trains were quite crowded many times throughout the summer, as people were not able to secure the gasoline needed for extensive automobile trips— not to mention the Sunday closing of filling stations.

As 1974 drew to a close, the Corporation saw the year as a year of solid progress highlighted by expanding services, the nation-wide reservation system, new equipment ordered or delivered and better on time performance.

The improved on time performance was attributal in part to the 150 new 3,000 horsepower diesel locomotives, the last 110 of which were delivered in 1974. This new power, along with new incentive— penalty contracts with a growing number of Amtrak's member railroads, finally broke the back of one of the Corporation's toughest early problems, late trains and unreliable schedules. In the final months of 1974, Amtrak trains were on time more than 80% of the time with substantial numbers of them operating in the 90% on time range. However, in 1978 the problem was again getting worse, especially on Con Rail routes.

Amtrak trains were more pleasant to ride in as well. By the end of the year, more than 1,035 of the older passenger cars had been overhauled and refurbished. Newly negotiated maintenance agreements, along with stricter supervision from Amtrak inspectors, resulted in improved equipment maintenance and cleanliness standards.

Equipment on order included seven more turbine trains based on the French design from an American firm. This would bring to a grand total of 13 five car turbine train sets, and plans were being made for still more car orders. And with the new trains, came new or refurbished stations. Some of these were East Lansing, Flint, and Port Huron in Michigan; Dubuque, Iowa; Lima, Ohio; Rockford, Illinois; and Fort Edward, Saratoga, and Plattsburg in New York state.

The reservation system (ARTS) was performing beautifully by the end of 1974, and had by December 31st handled over 18 million calls. The average time for each phone transaction had been reduced from 6½ to 3½ minutes. Passengers were finding fewer mistakes in reservations, and the corporation was profiting from better use of available space on its trains. Complaints about reservations, which a

year earlier had ranked third from the top in letters from passengers, were third from the bottom by the end of the year.

Track improvement was and is one of Amtrak's biggest problems in 1979. There are still many unresolved questions of legality, private versus public ownership and overlapping jurisdictions. However, Amtrak's Board of Directors approved spending $21.6 million to upgrade track between Boston and New York with more money to be allocated later to the Washington-New York section of the Northeast Corridor. Engineering studies began, and the first actual construction involved repairs to a draw bridge at Old Saybrook, Conn.

Reservations, track and equipment were not the only improvements Amtrak was making in its overall service. It began the new year in January, 1975 by reducing the minimum basic coach fare needed to qualify travelers for family plan discounts from $30 to $20. The effect was to bring many more medium-distance journeys into the range eligible for lower family fares. Family plan fares do not apply to trips beginning on Fridays or Sundays. In many cases, family plan fares are lower than any other public transportation available. Between Washington and Boston, for example, in 1975, a couple with two children (ages 2 through 11), could save $9.50 over the bus fares for a one way trip and $79.52 over the air coach fares. Family plan discounts apply to both coach and first class travel.

The biggest news however in early 1975 was the election of Mr. Paul H. Reistrup, Senior Vice President for Traffic of the Illinois Central Gulf Railroad, to be the Corporation's new President and Chief Executive Officer. He assumed Amtrak's top position on March 1st. Mr. Reistrup had been instrumental in making many passenger improvements and innovations on the Baltimore & Ohio and on the Illinois Central. He came to Amtrak, not only well grounded in rail passenger service, but also in other areas of railroading. Other positions he held with the B&O include that of assistant division engineer, general yardmaster, trainmaster and general superintendent— car utilization and distribution. Mr. Reistrup was well qualified to take over the nation's passenger service.

The next news item that gave credence that Amtrak was here to stay came on April 2, 1975. Amtrak announced that orders were placed with two U.S. manufacturers for 435 high performance cars at a cost of $235 million.

The largest new order went to Pullman-Standard Company at Chicago for a contract to build 235 double deck long distance cars. The second order was for the 200 Amfleet cars previously mentioned, the fourth of a series of orders to Budd for a grand total of 492 Amfleet cars. The full Budd order was completed by June, 1977 while the first bi-level cars

For several generations of passenger equipment, the standard equipment included an automatic coupler, an air brake line (the larger hose), the train signal line (the smaller hose) and the steam line (the large rigid pipe below the coupler). The system provided a communicating system from the conductor to the engineer, actually an air whistle system; an air brake system for the entire train and finally a means to move steam through the entire train for either heating or air conditioning.

This photo shows the entire system coupled together.

were to be delivered in early 1977, but did not arrive until late 1978 and 1979.

The Budd Amfleet cars were configured as coaches, cafe-coaches, club cars, club cafe coaches, coach dinette and two cars for lounge car service on the Montrealer. The cars were designed for short distance travel, but due to equipment shortages, the Amfleet can be found on a variety of long distance trains.

The bi-level cars will include coaches, dining cars, sleepers and lounge cars, and are to be used on long distance routes in the west.

Floor tracks, an important design feature, permit variable seat spacing and other configuration changes allowing Amtrak to maximize revenue as well as provide varying interior arrangements according to the needs of the market served. The result is that the Amtrak fleet, with these cars on order, will increase about 12% between 1975 and 1980 and the total seating and sleeping space available will go up about 84%. Altogether the order was the largest ever placed by one rail company since Canadian National ordered 389 cars in 1953.

Mid-1975 found Amtrak working on the track problems. A proposal for $700 million to start immediately for a national roadbed and track improvement program was strongly endorsed by Amtrak President Paul H. Reistrup. Responding to a House Commerce Subcommittee request for his ideas on a national roadbed, right-of-way, and track improvement program, Reistrup ticked off 17 locations across the country that would "get us off dead center" in halting the serious decline in the physical rail plant. The improvements would include lining and surfacing the existing track, installation of new ties, new rail and ballast, restoration or upgrading of alternative route segments for faster through service, improvements to signalling to permit higher speeds and to reduce interference from other traffic and the provision of grade-crossing protection or crossing eliminations. Reistrup said that the project would currently put unemployed skilled personnel back to work and take idle track equipment off the sidetracks. Amtrak could act as the government's prime contractor with the railroads as subcontractors. Reistrup added that the upgrading should be up to Federal Railroad Administration's Class 5 standards, which would allow speeds up to 90 miles per hour for passenger service.

Most of the track improvement program was on Conrail, and most of that on the former Pennsylvania Railroad sections.

In an effort to keep improving service, Amtrak and Canadian National signed a special agreement that enabled rail travelers from either Canada or the United States to purchase transportation on both national rail lines in a single transaction. The interline agreement permitted a CN or Amtrak passenger to purchase tickets for transportation and accommodation from his point of departure in Canada or the United States, to any American or Canadian city served by Amtrak or CN. The agreement took effect on September 15, 1975, and as of 1979, is still in effect for VIA Rail Canada.

Under the agreement, VIA and Amtrak reservation agents at central locations have access to the other company's computerized reservation system. Each can "acept inquiries and provide information to the general public regarding services, fares and reservations over the other's lines." Any authorized VIA travel agent in Canada can sell rail transportation over Amtrak lines. Any Amtrak ticket holding travel agent can sell transportation over VIA Canadian National or Canadian Pacific lines.

Amtrak also announced a USARail Pass for visitors from abroad in August, 1975. The pass offered unlimited coach class travel on Amtrak routes, and was originally sold only overseas through Amtrak appointed agents. Originally restricted to foreign nationals entering the U.S. on tourist, student or business visas, the USARail Pass is now open to everyone.

There were originally three types of passes as follows: $150 for 14 days, $200 for 21 days, and $250 for 30 days. In 1979 the USARail Pass was still one of the best travel bargains.

In an effort to investigate all possibilities for locomotive improvement, Amtrak announced in October, 1975 that it would lease a high-speed, lightweight Swedish electric locomotive to evaluate its performance for possible use in the Northeast Corridor. The unit was to be supplied by ASEA, a leading European locomotive manufacturer. The lease of the demonstration unit would permit Amtrak to properly evaluate advanced design and technology now embodied in state-of-the-art electric locomotives.

The Unit, model Rc4, differs from U.S. models by lightweight (180,000 pounds), about half of a comparable U.S. locomotive and its high horsepower, 6,000, with a four wheel design. The ASEA unit also uses an advanced thyristor control system, incorporating an "early warning" wheel slip control device which enables it to accelerate rapidly with relatively heavy loads to high speeds. The locomotive arrived in the U.S. in mid-1976, and testing has been completed and the locomotive returned to Sweden. See Chapter 3 for photos. Amtrak later ordered 15 high speed electric locomotives based on the Swedish design.

In late 1975, Amtrak and Auto-Train announced an important agreement, whereby Auto-Train would operate on Amtrak trains and over Amtrak routes. Auto-Train would continue to have complete jurisdiction over its sales, marketing, en route service and personnel. In 1977 the joint service (Flor-

idian) with Auto-Train was suspended and there were no further plans even in 1979.

Amtrak was caught very badly during the inflation squeeze during 1975-1979. It made a valiant effort to absorb a portion of the cost increases, but effective December 15, 1975 the Corporation raised most coach fares and some first class fares from 5 to 10% depending upon the route. A further increase of 5% took place on February 1, 1976, on a number of routes. These fare increases helped the situation somewhat, and apparently it did not injure patronage as that figure was again on the upswing by the end of 1975. Similar increases took place through 1979.

Ridership increases helped to secure Federal, State and Local support for station improvements and new construction. Federal agencies, with employment funding programs, states with rail improvement bonds, and cities with urban redevelopment projects have joined hands and are contributing millions of dollars toward passenger station refurbishment and new construction.

A major project in early 1976 was the $2.3 million program sponsored by the U.S. Department of Commerce and Transportation to clean up and repair eight rail passenger stations in the Northeast corridor. The program was initiated by the Commerce Department to provide employment for unemployed workers, and it was the Department of Transportation which earmarked the funds for station improvements. Amtrak and the Penn Central (later ConRail) were working with the Federal Railroad Administration to coordinate and perform the work.

Stations slated for the improvement were: Boston's South Station, Providence, Wilmington, Baltimore, New Haven, New London, Newark and Philadelphia's 30th Street Station. Improvements include cleaning and restoration of building exteriors, interior painting, signage and renevation of restrooms, platform paving and repair of canopies and overhaul of heating and lighting systems.

Improvements in the Northeast Corridor were not the only areas. In Illinois 21 stations were slated for improvement with the State paying 2/3's and Amtrak picking up the tab for 1/3. The work was performed by either the Burlington Northern or the Illinois Central Gulf.

In Michigan stations at Jackson, Ypsilanti, Ann Arbor and Chelsea were improved with State aid. At Kalamazoo, the station was converted to an intermodal facility with State and City assistance, and when completed turned out to be a boom for both the bus companies and Amtrak. These projects and others demonstrate that Amtrak, state agencies, bus lines and the railroads can cooperate for the common good of all.

Amtrak has also constructed a number of new

stations, such as at Jacksonville, Florida; Richmond, Virginia and St. Paul, Minnesota and elsewhere by 1979. Still others are in the planning stage.

Amtrak welcomes proposals from local governments for the rehabilitation of existing stations or the construction of new facilities, especially intermodal terminals.

Stations have been one of Amtrak's major problems, as too many of them were rundown and instead of being the railroad's best foot forward — where prospective customers first encounter rail service — they were descouraging and depressing. No wonder too many flew the next time.

The holiday period from December 17, 1975 through January 4, 1976 was not the big problem that Amtrak faced for several years, even though patronage was again moving upward from the same period in late 1974. Extra cars, 350 of them, from Amtrak's pool of existing equipment and the new Amfleet cars helped alleviate the equipment shortage, as well as cars borrowed from the Southern Railway and commuter cars from the Boston, New York, Philadelphia areas. Extra trains were also scheduled on certain days for the New York-Washington, New York-Miami and the Chicago-Detroit runs. This practice of leasing and borrowing equipment has continued through all of the holiday periods, and no doubt will continue to happen in the future providing some interesting train operations.

In September, 1977, Amtrak revised its pet policy after new federal regulations were issued that would have cost $13.8 million to comply with. Amtrak stopped carrying pets except for guide dogs accompanying blind passengers.

Car Maintenance took a big leap forward on January 16, 1976 when Amtrak assumed control of its first major maintenance base, the big Penn Central 12th Street coach yard and 16th Street locomotive shop in Chicago. Ownership has made it possible for Amtrak to invest its funds for equipment and capital improvements, and to consolidate work formerly done by three shops at Chicago into the one base. Greater efficiency and higher quality work will result.

As of early 1976, fifty Amtrak trains a day arrived and departed from Chicago and the former PC yard maintained 18 of them. Work done includes interior and exterior cleaning, mechanical and electrical inspections, plus watering and resupply. In addition, 12th St. is the assigned periodic maintenance point for 277 Amtrak cars.

Under the modernization plan, the work performed at the Burlington Northern yard was shifted to 12th St. (The company still leases the Santa Fe coach yards.) The upgraded facility has about 500 cars assigned to it, about 25% of the Amtrak fleet.

The new Amfleet equipment not only has the coupler, air brake system and communicating system line, but also electrical connections for heating and air conditioning, as well as lighting and other electrical systems. The entire train is dependent upon the locomotive for its electrical power, and no longer requires a steam line as was and is the case on much of Amtrak's conventional equipment. With the new Amfleet, Superliners and converted conventional equipment, train crews and passengers no longer need to worry about frozen steam lines during severe cold weather.

In addition, the Penn Central's commuter trains (now ConRail) are also maintained at the 12th St. Yard. Trains operating out of the north side of the Union Station over the Milwaukee Road continued to be maintained at the Milwaukee's Western Avenue shops.

During January and February, 1976, Amtrak took over the PC's Boston maintenance facilities at South Bay Yard and South Station, New Haven Diesel and Car shop, Philadelphia facilities at the Penn Coach Yard, 30th St. Station, and Race Street engine house; Harrisburg, Pa.; Detroit, Mich.; Buffalo, N.Y.; Rensselear, N.Y.; and various facilities in New York City and the Wilmington, Del. heavy repair shop. The Beech Grove Shops in Indiana were taken over by Amtrak during mid-1975.

As Amtrak took over the various shops and yards, it also began the maintenance work on the commuter cars owned by the local transit agencies and the Penn Central (now ConRail) mail train cars as well as its own equipment. At Buffalo, Amtrak also maintains passenger equipment for the Toronto, Hamilton and Buffalo Railroad.

Beginning March 1st, 1976, Amtrak made available their USARail pass to citizens of the United States, Canada and Mexico. The pass was also honored on Southern Railway. Children 2 through 11 pay one half an adult fare and the family plan is also available with the pass. Pass holders may upgrade any segments of their trips by paying the difference between regular coach fare and the desired Metroliner or first class service.

This move represented one more positive action on the part of Amtrak to improve sales and to provide the American public with a greater and more variety of service.

One month after Amtrak announced that the USARail pass would become available to North Americans, it announced that the pass would be offered through the peaktravel summer months at higher prices. The new prices for the domestic Rail Pass were $250 for 14 days of unlimited coach travel anywhere on the Amtrak system, $325 for 21 days and $400 for 30 days. The pass was (and is) good on all Amtrak trains except Metroliners and on all Southern Railway passenger trains. Winter prices were less expensive at $169, $219, and $259 respectively.

Other fare developments included excursion fares on many routes throughout the U.S.A. Such discounts ranged from 25 to 31% off the regular round trip coach fare. Some of the fares were part of a promotional campaign to encourage ridership on segments of routes, or at off peak times of the day, when ridership is usually low and there is plenty of space on the trains.

The 1976 Easter holiday travel surge was the first time since Amtrak took over in 1971 that they had enough additional equipment to operate 36 additional trains during the April 16-25 holiday period. Bolstering the fleet were nearly 200 new Amfleet cars already in service as well as new diesel and electric locomotives in the northeast and midwest. Additional cars were added on both the older conventional and new Amfleet runs. Since two of the higher capacity Amfleet cars can carry as many passengers as three older coaches, thousands of additional seats were available.

New equipment and expanded holiday travel is not enough to bring Amtrak out of the many problems still faced by the new company. Consequently, Amtrak began an experimental program to solicit new individual and group travel by train through the use of expanded staffs in the New York and Bensalem, Pennsylvania reservation centers. The additional agents were also available during peak telephone hours to more quickly answer public calls for information and reservations. Amtrak hired and trained 55 additional agents to place calls to thousands of travel agents, commercial accounts and organized travel clubs. Priority was given to promoting special travel packages, group moves, excursion fares and the U.S.A. Rail Pass. In mid-May, Amtrak added over 200 computer terminals in 90 stations giving more Amtrak agents direct access to the central computer. The result was additional business. Still not enough however, to benefit the system overall.

On June 15, 1976, the Corporation raised some fares by 5% on some routes to counter those rising operting costs not under Amtrak control and to help narrow the gap between revenues and deficits. Also, the long distance "Circle Fares" were cancelled and supplemented by the new U.S.A. Rail Passes good for unlimited coach travel.

As Amtrak rolled into its sixth year, life was getting more and more complicated. The U.S. Department of Transportation and the White House have not been favorable at all toward the National Railroad Passenger Corporation. The bus owners and operators were also becoming increasingly upset with Amtrak, and launched a major campaign against it. They zeroed in on the alleged "subsidized" fares on Amtrak trains. Amtrak President Paul Reistrup cited the fact that the bus industry is also subsidized since it does not have to pay its fair share of charges for highway usage.

Reistrup pointed out that the public highway system is paid only in part by user charges and the general taxpayers have shelled out $427 billion on the system. Of this amount, only $283 billion have been recovered in user charges. This leaves approximately $150 billion in the form of highway money derived from general taxation receipts. Thus, the bus industry has been heavily subsidized. Perhaps, the attitude of the bus industry critiquing Amtrak was only an admission that the rail carrier was succeeding in securing passengers from the bus lines. (This is a very important concept in transportation economics.)

In reality however, this would be a very poor objective, since the real objective is to secure passengers from the private automobile and on to public transportation. In order to really do this, the bus industry and Amtrak would have to work together, and the first sign of this appeared in a joint press release issued on June 24, 1976. It was announced that intermodal service was inaugurated on that day between New York City and New England by Amtrak and Greyhound. The new service allows travelers to buy one through ticket to or from designated New England points, be transferred at Boston's South Station to either transportation mode and have the convenience of baggage transfers routed through to destination.

At ceremonies held in New York's Penn Station, Charles D. Kirkpatrick, vice president-sales, Greyhound Lines and Al Michaud, vice president-marketing, Amtrak presented the first through bus-rail ticket to New England to representatives of city government.

Kirkpatrick called the new service a major transportation advance. It not only increased the mobility of travelers, but at the same time it offered a more fuel efficient travel alternative than other means of travel.

The inaugural trip was greeted by city and state officials in New Haven, Boston, Portsmouth and climaxed by a reception in Portland, Maine. Initially, Amtrak and Greyhound operated nine through schedules daily in each direction between New York and New England cities. Both companies stated that expansion of the intermodal concept could be expected in other areas of the United States in the future. As of 1978 this has not occurred.

As the summer moved toward the Bi-centennial celebration of July 4, Amtrak geared up for the heavy traffic over the holiday period. Extra cars operated on virtually every train in the nation and 14 extra trains operated in the New York-Washington and New York-Albany runs. Over 240 Amfleet cars were in operation. Business, overall, was running ahead of the previous year.

Another bit of progress was the elimination of "first class" rail transportation fare traditionally charged to sleeping and parlor car passengers in addition to their accommodation charges. On September 8, 1976, Amtrak first class and coach passengers paid the same rate for basic transportation corresponding to the existing coach fare. Sleeping car, parlor car (or Amclub) passengers pay an additional charge for the accommodations they reserve. It was pointed out that there was little change in what passengers actually pay for travel. New accommodation charges were adjusted upward to absorb the former first class fare differentials. For example, a passenger using a roomette between Chicago and Los Angeles paid a first class fare of $147 plus $35.50 for the sleeping car space, a total of $182.50. As of September 8th, the same trip still cost $182.50 but consists of $110.00 rail fare (same as the former coach class fare) plus $72.50 for the roomette in the sleeper.

The practice of charging higher "first class" fares dates back to the days when parlor and sleeping car space was provided by separate companies, such as the Pullman Company. The railroad sold transportation with higher per mile fares to passengers in the Pullman cars than it charged passengers in its own higher capacity coaches.

The only exception to Amtrak's simplified fare structure is the premium high speed Metroliner service in the Northeast Corridor, where a distinction between Metrocoach and Metroclub rail fares is still maintained.

As the July 4th Bi-centennial celebration drew to a close, Amtrak's biggest problem was the Department of Transportation. The DOT was withholding funds over a dispute over control of the Boston-Washington corridor trackage. By September, 1976, the amount was over $14 million in withheld operating funds. What the DOT wanted was to control the corridor trackage, which was to be purchased and rebuilt by Amtrak as of April, 1976 when Consolidated Rail Corporation took over the bankrupt northeast and midwest railroads.

Finally an agreement was signed between Amtrak and the DOT. Amtrak has given the federal government a lien on the property and the Federal Railroad Administration now has control over the design and reconstruction. With the new agreement, Amtrak received the withheld monies in early September and one more bridge was crossed in Amtrak's continuing struggle.

The history and development of Amtrak is an on-going one. Although this chapter brings us up to 1979, the history continues and will continue unless Congress, the railroad industry or Amtrak itself decides that there will be a different way to run passenger service. There is a need for rail service (both freight and passenger) in a balanced transportation system in the United States. Amtrak is struggling to take the first steps toward the fulfillment of that goal. The rest of this book is devoted to the trains, types of equipment and on board train services, throughout the United States and Canada.

This photo shows two Amfleet cars coupled together. Note the electrical jumper cables, the key to electrical life when the train is dependent upon the locomotive, which is known as HEP, **H**ead-**E**nd-**P**ower.

Amfleet and conventional equipment can be coupled together and operated in a train provided two things are done to the standard car. First, the car must be converted for Head-End-Power. And second, the diaphragm of the standard car must be modified (not necessarily replaced) to match the Amfleet diaphragm. This photo shows how the two types of equipment can match up.

As this is being written, conventional sleepers and coaches as well as other equipment are being converted for Head-End-Power for the Lake Shore and Broadway Limiteds. At least 25 sleepers have already been converted and are operating on a variety of Amfleet trains, such as the Pioneer, North Star, Inter-American, National Limited, Panama Limited, Montrealer and the Cardinal.

Chapter 3
Motive Power
A Pictorial Review

Amtrak's motive power history has been a *mixture* of hand-me-down locomotives from the railroads, to a number of rebuilt second-hand locomotives, to a series of massive SDP-40-F's; and finally to the demise of the "big fellows" only to be replaced by F40PH's. With the advent of ConRail, the motive power mix has become even more varied with freight GP-9's in bright orange color schemes as well as other power. As if this were not enough variety, the motive power also includes the immortal electric GG-1, which is now being slowly replaced by "boxy" looking double cab General Electrics.

Color schemes too have varied with the blunt arrow and later the wrap around candy stripe. All this has happened in less than a decade.

The following pages illustrate some of the wide variety found in Amtrak's stable.

During the early stages of Amtrak, passenger motive power carried the colors of the former owners, such as these Burlington Northern units exchanging places on the westbound North Coast Hi in Livingston, Montana. The units generally stayed fairly close to the original home road, but such was not always the case. (Jim Morin)

Switch engines are relatively rare on the Amtrak System, with most of the work being performed by the operating railroads. One Alco type S-2 is on the roster, and a small fleet of sixteen Electro-Motive Division SW-1's. Except for the S-2, painted in passenger colors, most of the SW-1's, such as 733 shown here at Wilmington, are simply Penn Central black with white lettering and numerals. Note the GG-I in the right hand corner in former Pennsy colors of Brunswick Green with Amtrak lettering. (J.W. Swanberg)

Along with other non-passenger power acquired with the ownership of the Northeast Corridor trackage, Amtrak received a number of GP-9's. Such units are being painted in the bright orange colors, and the same scheme is being applied to cabooses — only with a black roof. The 778 is a typical example of the GP-9 fleet. (J.W. Swanberg)

Amtrak owns 45 Alco RS-3's, a remarkable road-switcher by any yardstick. All are numbered in the 100 series (100 to 144) and serve on freight and work trains as well as switching service in some terminals, such as Chicago. As of early 1979, the units are Penn Central black, some undoubtedly will carry the new and cheery Amtrak bright orange. The 137 and 1337 are one and the same locomotive, with 137 being the current (1979) number. (J.W. Swanberg)

Amtrak owned a number of "F" units, such as the 105 and the 153, model F-7's from the Burlington Northern. The units were painted standard Amtrak colors of light grey, red nose and black roof. Almost all of the units came to Amtrak from either the BN or the Southern Pacific, and have since been retired. The 105 and 153 are leading the Puget Sound, about to depart Seattle for Portland over the BN's Pacific Division on September 14, 1973. (J.W. Swanberg)

Amtrak owns 12 of the remarkable FL-9's, a locomotive purchased from EMD by the New Haven for dual electric and diesel powered operation. Since Grand Central Station in New York City is "Electric" only, the former New York Central and New Haven lines were required to change to electric power at such locations as New Haven and Harmon. Looking for all the world like a standard stock F-9 model, the units are different and include such items as a third rail electric pick up shoe and a six wheel trailing truck. They did the job for which they were intended and eliminated the costly locomotive change. Amtrak has used them in passenger service, but the future is somewhat uncertain with the use of the Turboliners in New York State. (Amtrak)

For many years, the workhorse of the Amtrak fleet was the picturesque E-8's and E-9's. This former Seaboard Coast Line unit, now numbered 404, is probably closest to the E-9's as they were built; that is, with the fewest modifications. All four windows are in place, and wearing the original colors applied by Amtrak. The Electro-Motive product was one of the best looking passenger motive power designs ever built. (Amtrak)

Booster unit No. 472, type E9B, was former Milwaukee Road 33B and simply painted platinum mist without arrow or striping.

The E-8's and 9's have not been immune to changes. The 4317, later renumbered 323, has had some modifications made to the nose and has lost all of the porthole windows. The unit is at Harrisburg on Sept. 16, 1972. (J.W. Swanberg)

This side view of E-9, No. 425 shows the painting arrangements clearly. The 425 is moving train 75 through Harmon en route from New York to Albany on July 22, 1975 — pre-turboliner days. (J.W. Swanberg)

The first passenger locomotives purchased new by Amtrak were the controversial SDP-40F's from Electro-Motive in 1973. Massive 3000 horsepower locomotives, they eventually became implicated in a series of derailments and received severe speed restrictions on many railroads. Originally numbered 500 to 649 the locomotives served nation wide until they began to be phased out and rebuilt into F40PH's. (Amtrak)

The SDP-40F's were not around long enough to have many changes made to them, except some were repainted with the attractive wrap around candy striping, such as one can see on the 535 leading train 8, the Empire Builder, at Minneapolis in August, 1976. (Patrick C. Dorin)

The SDP-40F's ranged from San Diego to Boston and shared engine terminals with a variety of motive power. If one visited the New Haven terminal on October 13, 1974, this is the scene, a brand new SDP, the 600 on the left with an RDC, a GG1 and two Amtrak E-8's to the right. Note the different nose on the 600 as compared to the photo of the 535. (J.W. Swanberg)

Amtrak purchased 25 "P30CH's" from General Electric in 1974. The units, with head-end power, were originally designed for use with the Amfleet, but have been operated on other types of trains as well including Southern Pacific commuter service. The 708 is leading the 710 with Amfleet equipment for the Pacific Northwest service at the Minneapolis depot during the summer of 1976. The train to the right is the equipment for train 766, the former Arrowhead to Duluth. (Patrick C. Dorin)

The F40PH's from Electro-Motive are turning out to be one of the most reliable fleets of locomotives operated by the Amtrak System. Designed for the Amfleet and Superliners, the F units also team up with steam generator cars to handle conventional trains. The reader will note a small number below the cab window of the No. 233. That number indicates the former SDP-40F unit number which was dismantled and parts used to build a new F40PH, in this case, the 233, which is leading the old "Arrowhead" at Duluth, Minnesota's Union Station. (Patrick C. Dorin)

The immortal GG-1 continues on in 1979 in the fine
fashion of several decades of operation on the former
Pennsylvania Railroad. In the early days of Amtrak, it
was not uncommon to see the GG-1 in Penn Central
dress, such as the 4928 at Lancaster, Pennsylvania in
April, 1972. The 4928 is now owned by Amtrak and
has been renumbered 922 (Amtrak series 900 to 929).
(Patrick C. Dorin)

Amtrak 931 (now numbered 924) proudly displays the Amtrak colors of Platinum Mist, blue striping and brilliant red noses. This particular unit was built in 1943 and has seen a variety of services in the Northeast Corridor. (J.W. Swanberg)

General Electric has designed and built an electric locomotive that may eventually replace the GG-1. After all, nothing can last forever. The new E-60-CP's are numbered from 950 to 975, and are clean looking locomotives. They did have some initial operating problems, which have been largely solved. The 951 is shown here on the General Electric test track with a train of Amtrak passenger equipment. Note the dual gauge trackage. (Amtrak)

Amtrak tested a Swedish locomotive, known as the RC-4. Numbered X995, the unit proved fast and reliable and future locomotive designs will incorporate some of the Swedish features. The X995 had been nicknamed the "Swedish Meatball". (Amtrak)

A French electric locomotive was also tested in the Northeast Corridor, but did not do particularly well. Amtrak had numbered the unit X996 during the test period. In some ways, the French electric resembles the old Baldwin "Sharknoses". (Photo courtesy of Amtrak)

The most unusual lease arrangement made by Amtrak was of the Duluth, Missabe & Iron Range Railway passenger SD-9's. The DM&IR maintains two such units for passenger extras on its own line, and the lease was a natural for the Arrowhead. The color scheme of the Minnesota colors of maroon and gold even includes an arrowhead. The photo, taken in February, 1977, shows train 763 at Cambridge, Minnesota on the Burlington Northern's First Subdivision of the Wisconsin Division in automatic block signal territory. (Patrick C. Dorin)

During the past eight years of Amtrak history, a wide variety of locomotives have been leased or borrowed either on a long term, or for as short a period of even just one run. For example, Penn Central FL-9, No. 5049, powers train 73; enroute from New York to Buffalo. The FL-9 will come off at Harmon. The special blue and yellow unit, painted specifically for commuter service, was assigned to the New York area at the time the photo was taken in November, 1974. (J.W. Swanberg)

Switching service is performed by the contracting railroads, such as the Santa Fe pulling the Southwest Limited from the Chicago Union Station for servicing. The 542 is a rare Fairbanks, Morse type H-12-44 TS, designed especially for the Santa Fe complete with steam generator for passenger train switching in Chicago. (J.W. Swanberg)

Santa Fe crews have also used GP-20's, such as the 3138 shoving the former "Super Chief" into the Chicago Union Station during August, 1971. Amtrak was still very young, and the Santa Fe F-7 units were also very prominent on what was once the Texas Chief and Super Chief/El Capitan.

Amtrak, on at least one occasion, operated the San Francisco Zephyr behind steam. Union Pacific 4-8-4, No. 8444 on February 14, 1975 led the San Francisco Zephyr as Extra 8444 West between Denver and Cheyenne over the First Subdivision of the Wyoming Division in CTC territory. Coupled to two SDP-40F's, the 621 and 585, the twelve car train is doing 45 miles per hour through Brighton, Colorado. Rail photographer Richard Kindig captured the historic event on film for all to enjoy for years to come.

Steam generator cars are essential when conventional trains are powered by either the EMD F40PH's or the General Electric P30's. As the "E" units were released from service as the new power arrived on the scene, some were converted to steam generator cars, such as the 670 coupled to two F40PH's. The motive power combination is awaiting the arrival of the Empire Builder at St. Paul during the fall of 1978. (Patrick C. Dorin).

Steam generator car 662 is a former Burlington Northern diesel, type "F" unit reconstructed for steam service. This equipment operates with the EMD "F40PH's" to provide steam for conventional equipment. The 662 was photographed in train 18, the North Coast Hiawatha, at St. Paul in January, 1979. (Patrick C. Dorin)

In late 1978 and early 1979, Amtrak is still securing second hand power. Generally, the units are pressed into service with a new number and a simple "Amtrak" stenciled on. Geep 763, obviously a former Union Pacific unit, had yet to receive its new orange color scheme when photographed at the Santa Fe coach yards in Chicago, February 3, 1979. (Patrick C. Dorin)

A number of E-8 and E-9 diesel units have been modified by Amtrak for electrical head-end power, replacing the original steam generator. The units can handle Amfleet, bi-level and the new single level cars that are in the planning stage as of early 1979. The units are also receiving the wrap around striping. It is interesting to note that EMD's "E" type passenger diesels are surviving far longer than other diesel passenger power built during the same era. This particular train was assembled by Amtrak for publicity photos not only for the Amfleet equipment (note the two cafe-coach-club cars) but also for the rebuilt motive power. (Amtrak)

As for foreign power in early 1979, Amtrak will obviously continue to use it. Conrail 8478 (SW 1, 600 horsepower switcher) with a Conrail crew assembles train 50, the Cardinal on February 3, 1979. The train is still minus its baggage car, which will be added at the Chicago Union Station. The steam in the background of the 12th Street coach yards will soon be a sight of the past, as all equipment will be built or converted to electric "head-end power". (Patrick C. Dorin)

Alco RS-3, Amtrak 117 is the former Penn Central 5441, and as of February, 1979 was assigned to switching the Santa Fe coach yards in Chicago. Complete with number boards, the RS-3 will look distinctive in Amtrak's bright orange dress. (Patrick C. Dorin)

During emergencies, the operating railroads will frequently assign an extra locomotive to the Amtrak power consist. Such was the case on a January, 1979 Sunday when the BN assigned F-45, No. 6636, to train 18. The unit was taken off the train at St. Paul and is shown here waiting for the North Coast to depart for Chicago so it can proceed to a BN engine terminal. (Patrick C. Dorin).

Not only did Amtrak lease power to the Southern
Pacific, but also Conrail got into the act. A pair of
Conrail suburban trians between Chicago and Valpa-
raise in early 1979 were assigned a single F40PH and
three former bi-level C&NW 400 coaches. The train is
shown at Valpo on February 3, 1979. (Patrick C. Dorin
and Frank Schnick).

Amtrak not only leases power, but also loans it out. For example, several General Electric P30's were loaned to the Southern Pacific for commuter train service in 1978. The 707 is shown here after arrival in San Francisco with a commute train from San Jose on December 27, 1978. The big General Electrics were assigned to the double deck coach trains only, since they are self-contained and do not necessarily require a steam generator. (Thomas Dorin).

The newest railroad in 1978 to become involved with Amtrak operations is the Minnesota Transfer. The MTR switches the new "Midway Depot" at St. Paul. The 304 was assigned to the depot the day this photo was taken in late January, 1979. (Patrick C. Dorin).

Chapter 4
Amtrak Accommodations and Equipment: A Wonderful Way to Travel

The coach, sleeping car and parlor car, now referred to as the club car, are the revenue producers for any passenger train operation. The design, comfort and fare charged as well as the attitudes of the crew determines whether or not a passenger will return for another trip.

Amtrak's equipment has been, and still is in many ways, a variety of hand-me-down cars from the nation's railroads and far too many were in worn out condition. It is the purpose of this chapter to review the various accommodations and equipment offered to the traveling public, both the old and the new. The chapter is divided into three sections covering coaches, sleeping cars and last but not least, the club cars.

Coach and Chair Cars

The backbone of Amtrak service is the coach and chair car service offered on every single train operated by the Amtrak System. As of late 1979 Amtrak did not operate a single All-Sleeping Car or an All-Parlor Car train anywhere on its system lines.

Basically there are four types of coach accommodations found on Amtrak trains. The most common is the day coach seat, which consists of a reclining back, soft cushions and generally a foot rest. The next type is a variation of the day coach seat but with the addition of a leg-rest. This is sometimes known as a day-night coach. The third type of accommodation is a non-reclining seat, usually with a walk over back that can reverse directions by being moved from one side of the cushion to the other. These are sometimes known as commuter or suburban car seating, and offered primarily in rail diesel car or Silverliner equipment. The fourth type is actually the most luxurious type of coach accommodations ever offered on the American railroads, and that is the slumbercoach. The slumbercoach is a private room that is more compact than a roomette, and offers armchair seating by day and a soft cu-

shioned bed at night. There are two types of slumbercoach accommodations, single and double rooms, both of which offer complete toilet and washbasin facilities. These four types of accommodations are offered in ten different types of coaches operated over Amtrak System lines.

The most common coaches are of course, the day coaches, which range in capacity from 40 to 84 passengers depending upon the type and original railroad owner. The interior configurations vary with the smaller capacity cars including large men's and women's dressing rooms or lounges, and with the higher capacity cars being equipped with only small washrooms for the different sexes. A number of the day coaches from the Burlington and the Wabash (now Burlington Northern and Norfolk & Western respectively) are equipped with domes, such as the Twin Cities Zephyr cars and the Blue Bird equipment. In all instances, day coaches are equipped with reclining seats and most have foot rests. There are some combination baggage coach cars with smaller seating capacities. Day coach equipment is operated on all trains, except for the multiple unit (RDC, electrics, Metroliners) equipped trains.

The second most frequent category is the day-night coaches, which range in capacity from 44 to 48 seats. In this case, the seats have leg rests and all are equipped with large dressing room lounges at each end of the car for men and women. Many of these cars are dome cars from such famous streamliners (domeliners) as the California Zephyr, Empire Builder, North Coast Limited and Denver Zephyr. In this case, the large dressing rooms were located beneath the dome instead of the ends of the car.

The interior decor of Amtrak coaches in these two categories was most attractive. Walls and floors were carpeted for noise reduction as well as an attractive motif. (Not all coaches had floor carpeting.) Seats were upholstered with a similar color as the walls, floor and ceilings, which were done

In the beginning, not a single passenger car or locomotive carried the Amtrak colors. It would be a while before the leased and purchased equipment would be repainted. Furthermore, equipment strayed far and wide from the original home road and created numerous electrical and mechanical problems for car repairmen not familiar with the equipment. This Seaboard Coast Line coach is on the old Penn Central at Lancaster, Pennsylvania (not too far from home) and is in relatively good shape. Such could not be said about all equipment during those early days in 1971. (Patrick C. Dorin).

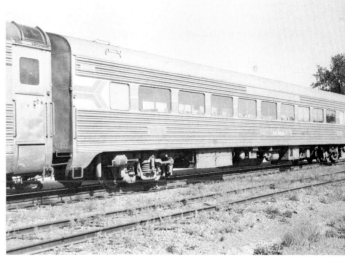

As business increased, Amtrak became more and more desperate for equipment. Funding has always been slow and controversial and the company turned to the railroads for additional cars. One example, the Burlington Northern loaned a number of former C&NW "400", Great Northern (never painted BN's green and white) coaches to the passenger carrier. This coach is in the consist of the Arrowhead at Cambridge, Minnesota in October, 1975. (Patrick C. Dorin).

One can tell the passenger capacity of conventional coaches by the first two digits of the car number. For example, coach 7200 shown here, has a capacity for 72 passengers. The 7200 is the former Northern Pacific 527, and the Missouri-Kansas-Texas, 1202R, the J. Pinckney Henderson built by Pullman in 1954. This photo was taken in August, 1976.

up in greens, blues, tans, yellows and cream colors. The seats were often done in floral arrangement which was most pleasing to the eye.

Amtrak's Metroliners are probably the most sophisticated of the coach equipment operating anywhere in North America. Conceived in the early 1960's for a high speed passenger train service over the former Pennsylvania Railroad between Washington, D.C., and New York City, the new equipment was originally scheduled to be placed in service in 1967. However, bugs by the millions plagued the cars, and when Amtrak took over in 1971, Penn Central was operating only a limited Metroliner service.

The Metroliner coaches, known as Metrocoach, are designed for multiple unit operation in pairs. Each coach has a capacity of 76 passengers with reclining seats and carpeted floors. The interior decor is done in various colors including brown and greens punctuated with simulated wood grain bulkheads. Each seat has its own individual reading light beamed down from above baggage racks. The windows are a bit small, but do not interfere with the viewing of the passing scenery. The interior reminds one of an airliner but with larger windows and better seating. The cars are smooth running despite the problems with former Penn Central track-

age at the time of this writing. The only drawback, if it can be called a drawback, is the vibration of the pantographs on the overhead catenary at crossovers.

Metro Snack-Bar coaches have a seating capacity of 60 passengers with the same type of seating as the full coach. Rest rooms are located at the non-cab end of each car with one on each side of the aisle. This is the case with both types of coaches. Electrically, the Metroliners are probably the most complicated unit equipment yet built by the USA. The trains are very popular, and passengers that this writer has interviewed state that they enjoy the interior decor and the dependability of rail travel as the primary reasons for going *Metroliner* again and again when traveling in the Northeast Corridor.

Still another multiple unit car operated by Amtrak is the "Silverliner." Silverliners are commuter coaches, primarily operated on Harrisburg-Philadelphia runs, with bright interiors and a nonreclining 3-2 seating arrangement. The cars generally have a seating capacity of about 125 passengers. There is nothing fancy about the equipment, but the comfort index is excellent for the distance and time passengers spend aboard.

Rail Diesel Cars are also operated by Amtrak on a few runs either in the Northeast or in the Midwest.

Amtrak coach 7251 is another 72 passenger car, which was rebuilt from the former New Haven parlor car, the Stamford. The rounded roof indicates the car was once part of the famous American Flyer fleet built for the New Haven and other railroads by Pullman. (J.W. Swanberg)

Coach 6452 accommodates 64 passengers, and it too was once part of the MKT's "Texas Special" as well as having been sold to the Northern Pacific. (Patrick C. Dorin).

Amtrak has refurbished the RDC's with the installation of new airline-type seats with snack trays, floor and wall carpeting for noise suppression, complete rewiring and rebuilding of engines, torque converters and major components to new-car standards for increased reliability. Amtrak once owned 24 Rail Diesel Cars.

The Turbo Trains, formerly operated between New York City and Boston, were the only dome-liners running in the Colonial Corridor, and they were indeed quite the trains. The Turbo's were described in detail in Chapter 22 of THE DOME-LINERS, published by Superior Publishing Company in 1973. The trains offered day coach seating with reclining backs, fold down tables, indirect lighting, carpeting and draperies. Meal and beverage service was provided by a specially designed galley bar, and dome seating was similar to the coach seating. The original three car sets have since had equipment added to them and Amtrak operated two five cars sets and one four car set. All three sets have been withdrawn from service. VIA Rail Canada is still, in 1979, operating their Turbo Trains.

The Turboliner, however, has turned out to be the most popular of the two types of turbine powered coach trains in the USA. Altogether there are 13 five car sets in service. These new trains represent a second and third generation version of a turbine train series which has logged millions of miles of revenue service in France with a very high reliability and passenger acceptance. The trains are capable of sustained speeds of up to 125 miles per hour on conventional track and consistently operate up to that speed in France. Lower speeds, of course, are observed by Amtrak either because of track conditions or the ICC imposed 79 miles per hour limit on Automatic Block Signal equipped trackage.

The French call the trains RTG for "rame a turbine a gaz" or gas turbine train and to distinguish it from the first generation French turbos which used a combination of diesel and turbine power and were called "ETG." These turbine trains are designed to provide high-speed, comfortable coach service over medium distances. Interior appointments are designed for this type of market.

The first generation French turbine train went into service in 1970. In the first two years of their operation on the Paris-Caen-Cherbourg run, French National Railways reported they had operated more than five million miles with a high degree of reliability and with a 25% increase in ridership over the service they replaced.

The RTG is a five car train with a power unit at each end. The total train length is 423 feet. All five cars, including the power units, provide day coach seating with reclining backs. The interior decor includes draperies, large windows and trays for each seat. The first two Turboliners included table seating in the center bar-grill-coach car, but subsequent trains did not include such seating. The trains have been extremely popular in the USA, especially on

Coach 6805 (for 68 people) has led quite a history. Originally an observation car (Priest River) for the GN's Empire Builder, it was rebuilt as a sleeper with a small lounge area, and then completely re-constructed as a full coach in 1968. The car was already 21 years old by the time of its conversion to coach service. Photographed in 1975 at Seattle, the car had been in service over the Southern Pacific and was still carrying the red mars light and back up light on the safety gate. (Patrick C. Dorin).

Coach 5261 reflects the wide variety of equipment that could (and can) be found on the Amtrak System. The former C&O car has a completely different window arrangement accommodating the divided coach sections within the car. The car is operating in thru Chicago — Washington service on the Broadway Limited at Harrisburg, Pennsylvania in this October, 1975 photo. (Patrick C. Dorin).

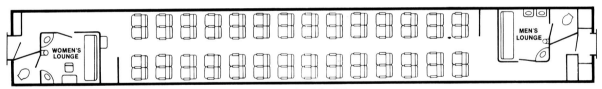

EXAMPLE OF COACH

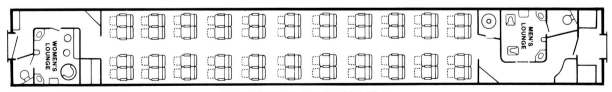

EXAMPLE OF LEG-REST COACH

the Chicago-Detroit run where patronage has sky-rocketed since they have been placed in that service.

The new Amfleet coaches have signaled the end of the dark ages of USA passenger car development. The new stainless steel car incorporates a number of advanced comfort and convenience features including electric heating and air conditioning, reclining day coach seats with individual tray tables, improved ride characteristics and newest federal safety features. All of the cars (492 Amfleet cars— almost 8 miles of gleaming stainless steel equipment) are capable of being pulled by either electric or diesel locomotives and can operate at speeds up to 120 miles per hour. Thermal and acoustical insulation provides an exceptionally quiet interior and minimizes the transfer of heat through the car body. There are two types of full coaches, reclining 84 seat cars and leg rest 60 seat cars for overnight travel.

Interiors are flexible to meet changing markets. For example, seats are mounted on floor tracks so that spacing can be varied for cars operating on long, intermediate or short distance runs.

The Amcoach seats are designed for maximum relaxation. Each seat is wider than first class aircraft seats, richly upholstered and fully reclining with spacious center arm rests, with fold down tables for seat side dining. There are individual adjustable reading lights above the seats.

An example of the interior of the Amfleet is as follows: The bulkheads are dark brown carpet and the extremity of the car closest to the vestibule, adjacent to the lavatories is reddish-orange metal. The ceiling is silver above the aisle with light gray carpet above the luggage racks, the bottom of which are white leatherette. Walls above and below are white plastic. The smallish windows are set in black plastic edged with stainless steel. Dark brown carpet covers the lower walls. Floor carpeting is wine-colored with black wavy lines. Seat backs are dark brown and have fold out tables and net bags for storing small items. The headrests are purple, and the remainder of the seats are a mixture of purple, orange, red and brown in a flowered pattern. Automatic sliding doors provide entry into the cars from the vestibule. Lighting is a combination of bullet and flourescent (indirect). Seated adjacent to a window, it is difficult for one to see out of the windows across the aisle. From the aisle seats, one has a little better visibility. The riding quality is good but the noise level seems to be a little high for newly designed equipment.

All Amfleet cars include sound facilities for taped music, train announcements and crew communications.

The interiors are color coordinated (as previously mentioned) with carpeting, fluorescent lighting, and tinted windows. The cars are 85 feet, 4 inches

Dome coach No. 9400, the Silver Castle, was originally a flat top coach reconstructed by the Burlington in June, 1949 to the identical design of the first dome coach (also rebuilt by the Burlington) in June, 1945. Sometimes referred to as "pattern domes" the two cars were truly historic and both saw service with Amtrak. Silver Dome (the first car) was ironically numbered 9401 by Amtrak. The "Silver Castle" was photographed in the consist of the Arrowhead at Cambridge in August, 1976. (Patrick C. Dorin).

Dome cars were numbered by Amtrak in the 9000 series. This particular dome coach, the 9560, is also a historic car, having been part of the world famous Wabash "Blue Bird". Originally Wabash No. 200, the Norfolk and Western renumbered the car 1610. The car has operated in both long and intermediate distance train service, and is shown here in the consist of old train 9, the North Coast, at Billings, Montana in September, 1973. (J.W. Swanberg)

Amtrak 9455, the Silver Saddle, has a capacity of 46 passengers and was once assigned to the Burlington's California Zephyrs. The car was photographed carrying the markers of train 763, the old Arrowhead, a train which seemed to carry a wider variety of equipment than any other train in the Amtrak System. October, 1975, Cambridge Minnesota. (Patrick C. Dorin).

Dome car 9479 is also a transcontinental, leg rest coach, and comes to Amtrak from the Burlington Northern as former NP552. The former BN domes continued to serve on the Empire Builder, North Coast Hi and even the San Francisco Zephyr through 1979. The 9479 is shown here at the BN coach yard in Seattle in March, 1975. Domes provided an unique travel experience, and one could look up, down and all around, especially in the short domes, which provided excellent "see-ahead" visibility. The decision to eliminate "domes" from the passenger train of the 1980's has not been well received, and it is hoped that Amtrak will reconsider the dome in future orders.

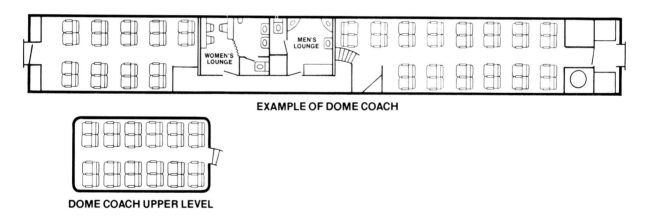

EXAMPLE OF DOME COACH

DOME COACH UPPER LEVEL

long; 10 feet, 6 inches wide; 12 feet, 8 inches high; and weigh 106,000 pounds. These new coaches are definitely Amtrak's new generation. However, the new Amcoaches are only part of Amtrak's new coach equipment story. But before we get into Amtrak's new Bi-level equipment, we must back track and take a look at Amtrak's former "400" and El Capitan equipment.

Amtrak's first exposure to double deck equip-

ment was with the operation of the former El Capitan equipment on Amtrak's Chicago-Los Angeles train service. This equipment, with reclining leg-rest seats, still ranked in 1975 as the finest long distance "day-night" equipment ever constructed and operated on American railroads. The equipment has always been popular with passengers, and the Santa Fe is to be commended for its innovation. The Santa Fe referred to the El Capitan as

Observation cars rank quite high on the travel experience scale, and Amtrak has a small fleet from the various railroads. However, they do not always operate to the best possible advantage. Coach observation car No. 3870 is a former New York Central "Parlor Observation" car refurbished by Amtrak for coach service. The car is serving as the lead car of train 365, the Blue Water, arriving in Chicago on May 26, 1976. (J.W. Swanberg)

"Hi-Level" and it was this equipment that provided Amtrak with the seed for new ideas in the creation of new long distance passenger equipment.

Meanwhile, as the Santa Fe was experiencing success with its hi-level equipment on the transcontinental routes, the Chicago and North Western was ordering Bi-level equipment from Pullman-Standard for its Flambeau and Peninsula 400's. Not only were the new cars a new innovation in coach design but they also incorporated electric heating and air conditioning.

Amtrak leased the former 400 bi-level equipment for short runs in the mid-west, and the experience gained with the intermediate distance bi-level day coaches and the long distance hi-level day-night cars provided Amtrak with the data required for ordering new bi-level cars from Pullman-Standard in 1975.

The new Amtrak bi-level coaches feature seats spaced as far apart or further than first-class airline seats with reclining back and foot or leg rests. Folding tray tables are mounted behind each coach seat, and there are luggage storage areas above and under the seats. Entry into the bi-level is through a wide central door (on each side) on the lower level, rather than the traditional stairway and door at each end. A stairway connects upper and lower levels. The entrance of each full coach and sleeping car also has fold out ramps, wide aisles and handrails to allow unassisted mobility and access to all facilities on the lower levels by handicapped travelers, including those using wheelchairs.

The capacity of the coaches is 77 for long distance travel. The cars are constructed of stainless steel and incorporate air suspension systems that smooth out the ride, and heavy acoustical insulation dampens both exterior and interior sounds.

As with the Amfleet, heating and air conditioning is electric powered from the locomotive. Seats are also mounted on special floor tracks running the length of the car interior to permit variable seat spacing to meet different marketing needs. The bi-level cars are 85 feet long, 10 feet, 2 inches wide and 16 feet, 2 inches high. The weight of each coach is 157,000 pounds. The interior decor is based on Southwest Indian artistic design.

The new bi-level equipment represents Amtrak's greatest step forward in the modernization of the coach fleet throughout the United States. One can say that the cars fit the two basic styles in operation since 1971, the day service and the day-night service which is what all Amtrak coach equipment provides. Amtrak originally ordered 102 coaches and 42 coach baggages with baggage section on the lower level. At the time of this writing in February,

1979, it was believed that the bi-levels would be in service by the fall season.

Coach travel is by far the most important of the train service offered by Amtrak and the member railroads. Coach patronage makes up over 96% of Amtrak business, with the sleeping and club car business dividing up the remaining 4%. Travel by Amtrak coach, be it conventional day or daynight, Amcoach, Metroliner, Slumbercoach, Silverliner, RDC, Turbo or Turboliner, or Superliner is a very fine way to see the U.S.A. for real — by rail.

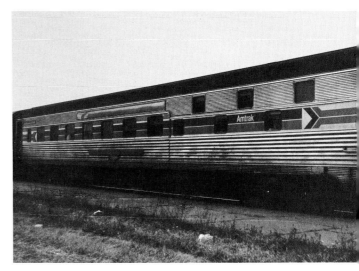

Slumbercoaches have the distinction of having the most beds ever in a standard size passenger car. The 24 single, 8 double room car can accommodate 40 passengers. The original concept of the slumbercoach, offering a private room at coach fare, went into service on the Burlington in 1956 on the then new Denver Zephyr. About the same time, the Baltimore and Ohio began offering the service on the All-Coach Columbian. A short time later, the Northern Pacific and the Missouri Pacific joined the slumbercoach club with the stainless steel beauties from the Budd Company and Pullman operated. (A. Robert Johnson)

Still another railroad, the New York Central, invested in Budd Slumbercoaches, and liked the 24-8 cars so well, it designed still another slumbercoach, known as the 16-10 — or 16 single rooms, 10 double rooms for a passenger capacity of 36 passengers. The New York Central cars were purchased by Amtrak (numbered 2000 to 2006) and operated on a variety of trains to Florida and the West Coast as well as the Broadway Limited. The 2004, shown here, is in service on train 40 at Gary, Indiana in January, 1973. (Patrick C. Dorin).

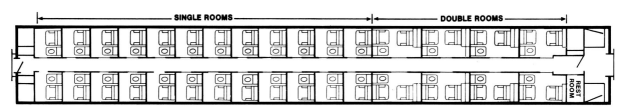

EXAMPLE OF SLUMBERCOACH

Sleep and Travel

Have you ever had the experience of lying in a nice crisp bed with warm blankets as a gentle rain beats against the window in an uneven rhythm? Add to that combination of a cozy atmosphere of a train traveling across the country at nearly 80 miles per hour and the gentle motion of the car, the rain and the sounds of the whistle up ahead and you are lulled to sleep on the finest way to travel known to man - sleeping car travel.

Sleeping car travel in the United States, Canada and Mexico was, and still is, synonomous with the Pullman Company. Indeed, Amtrak sleepers are still unofficially referred to as "Pullmans".For many years Pullman operated the finest sleeping car services to be found anywhere in the world. North American travel was un-doubtedly the best, and few countries could match what could be ridden from Mexico to Alaska. And Amtrak carries on that fine tradition of sleeping car travel on a number of routes throughout the United States. In fact, Amtrak offers sleeping car services on all but a few routes, such as Chicago - Port Huron, Chicago - Detroit and other short haul routes.

Amtrak offers four basic sleeping accommodations. First is the roomette, designed for one person and includes a bed that lowers or folds down from the wall and complete toilet and wash basin facilities. Roomette accommodations are sold in either standard roomettes or the duplex roomette.

The second accommodation is the bedroom, which is designed for two people with an upper and lower berth and complete toilet and wash basin facilities. Amtrak bedrooms are former compartments and double bedrooms, as they were originally designated. There are several variations of bedrooms, some with a full length sofa perpendicular to the side of the car, others with a single seat sofa with an arm chair that can be moved about, while still others are simply equipped with two chairs. Toilet facilities are fully enclosed.

The third accommodation is the bedroom suite, which is actually nothing more than two bedroom together with their common wall folded back for family or large group travel. The bedroom suite accommodates four passengers.

The last accommodation offered by Amtrak is the drawing room. Such rooms provide accommodations for three people and includes a variety of seating arrangements including at least one sofa. While the sofa provides one bed, there is also a lower and upper berth. Again washroom facilities are fully enclosed.

Almost all of the Amtrak sleeping car fleet is made up of the very popular 10 roomette, 6 bedroom cars, while a substantial number of other cars are combinations of roomettes and bedroms, 11 or 12 bedroom cars and 7 or 8 bedroom, 3 drawing room cars. There are other combinations to be sure, but the bulk of the sleeping car fleet falls into these categories.

The interiors of Amtrak sleepers are second to none. Carpeting is used throughout including the walls and bulkheads in many cases. Bright colors are used, such as greens, yellow, blues, purples, reds and many combin-ations. Upholstery is generally flowered with various colors that complement the colors in the aisles. Al-together the entire atmosphere is a restful one, and the tradition of sleeping car travel is being carried on in the grand manner of USA railroading.

The new double deck sleeping cars offer sleeping accommodations for one to four passengers in accommodations similar to the ones in service for decades. The new equipment is to be used on transcontinental runs to the Pacific Coast and possibly the overnight runs to New Orleans and elsewhere.

The design of the new sleepers posed a number of problems for Pullman-Standard that were quite different from those encountered in other rail car designs. Since the decline of long distance rail travel in the mid-1950's, there was no known research on the preferences of sleeping car passengers.

To determine the preferences of the modern day traveler, Pullman Standard engineers carried out a complete research program involving several steps. This led to a series of mock-ups constructed of plywood with foam seats and bed cushions to allow people to actually test the convenience and comfort of the cars. A variety of people participated in the study - all volunteers from Pullman Standards Champ Carry Technical Center. They ranged in height from 5' 1" to more than 6' 6" with waist sizes from 23" to 46". Volunteers included men and women, married couples and singles.

The survey was not statistical in nature, but more of an opinion poll. The travelers were asked to imagine that they were entering the compartments for a long distance trip. They tried out the accommodations, making themselves at home. Some were given luggage to unpack and store, while all raised and lowered the beds and seats, tested the convenience of hide-a-way tables and experimented with other features of the cars. They were then questioned about the convenience of the compartment and asked for ideas concerning changes they thought were necessary. A number of modifications were made in the sleepers as a result of the study.

The sleeping car designs call for four-person "family units" and two-person staterooms. All quarters feature comfortable adjustable seats, ample rooms for storing luggage and other items, sliding doors, large windows for viewing the passing countryside and spacious bedding. The sleeping cars are also equipped with a specially designed room for handicapped trvelers. The room is large enough for a person in a wheelchair to be comfortable and includes special washfoom facilities.

There are 70 bi-level sleepers on order with a sleeping capacity of 44 passengers in the 14 economy rooms, 5 deluxe bedrooms, 1 family room and 1 special bedroom car configuration. These are the first all new sleeping cars built in nearly two decades, although a number of sleepers were rebuilt from the floor up for the Santa Fe and Union Pacific during the 1960's. The new sleepers insure the continuation of Amtrak's first class service on the long distance routes.

CLUB & PARLOR CARS

Amtrak has operated only three basic types of parlor car services, and that operation has been relatively limited in scope. Parlor, or club service as it is now called, was originally offered only in the Boston - Washington runs, the Hiawatha and the Abe Lincoln.

Three types of parlor cars were operated by Amtrak. The first was the streamlined parlor car purchased from the railroads. Some of these were former dome parlor cars, but most were flat top cars from the New Haven or Penn Central. This equipment was fully carpeted with single seating on each side of the aisle. The second type is the Metroclub. These are the Metroliner parlor cars, equipped with a galley for food service and single seating. The newest type are the Amclub cars for the new Amfleet. These full parlor cars feature the popular Canadian style 2-1 seating with a first class capacity of 33 passengers.

The original Amclub car service was part of a combination cafe and coach with the serving bar separating the coach and club sections. The club car attendant has access to the food service area to serve his passengers at their seats.

Club car service is designed to give the passenger more for his extra fare. They have softer seat fabrics, thicker seat cushions, extrawide armrests and a deeper recline position. They arealso wider than the coach seat.

Colors chosen for the Amclubs include brown, blue and black tweed for the carpeting, and a plush deep red for the seats. Other seat colors include red, purple and deep blue.

Experience gained with the Amclubs was incorporated into the new Turboclub on the new New York-Buffalo trains. The Turboclub is similar to the Amclub but the seats are slightly narrower because of the narrower car frame.

According to Amtrak, the high occupancy rate for the Metroclub demonstrates there is still a demand for club or parlor car service. The tradition of parlor car travel began when the New Haven inaugurated their all parlor car train, "Merchants Limited". It is the intent of Amtrak to offer a full spectrum of service - to be like a fully stocked store where a customer may shop for either economy or luxury.

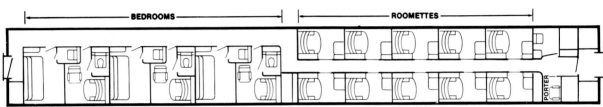

EXAMPLE OF 10-ROOMETTE, 6-BEDROOM SLEEPER

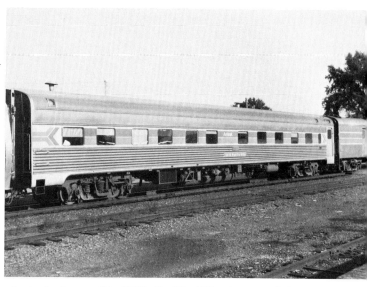

The Union Pacific Budd built 10 roomette, six double bedroom sleepers were among those cars at the top of the list for Amtrak purchase in 1971. The cars were operated system wide, and along with other roomette-bedroom cars became the backbone of the Amtrak sleeping car fleet. This UP 10-6 sleeper is carrying the markers for "First No. 2" en route from Denver to Chicago in July, 1971. (Patrick C. Dorin).

Amtrak sleeper No. 2515, Pacific Hills, is part of the former Union Pacific "Pullman" fleet. It is one of a growing fleet of cars going through a rebuilding program that includes electrical power for heating (instead of steam) and air conditioning. Pacific Hills is part of the consist of the North Star en route from Chicago to Duluth, Minnesota during the summer of 1978. (Patrick C. Dorin).

Another former Union Pacific sleeper, the 11 double bedroom Star Bay, is also in Amtrak service. the UP "Star" series were rebuilt from other equipment in 1965. This particular car was the former 5 double bedroom lounge, the "Cedar City". (J.W. Swanberg)

Amtrak Sleeper 2261, the Placid Harbor, in the consist of old No. 9, the North Coast Hi, at Billings, Montana during December, 1976.

Sleeper No. 2264, the Placid Meadow (from the Union Pacific Placid Series) is an 11 double bedroom car that has literally run nationwide. The car was repainted during the summer of 1978 with the striping consistent from one end of the car to the other. No more blunt arrow! The photo was taken in October, 1978 at St. Paul and the car is being switched into the consist of a Burlington Northern passenger extra. (Patrick C. Dorin).

Still another example of Amtrak sleeping cars is the Indian Maid, a former Santa Fe 11 double bedroom sleeper. The car is shown here in the consist of train 14, the Coast Starlight in December, 1978. (Patrick C. Dorin).

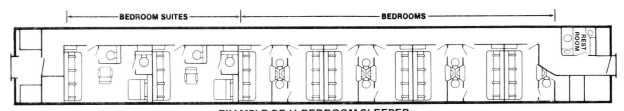

EXAMPLE OF 11-BEDROOM SLEEPER

Southern Railway, "Potomac River", a 10-6 sleeper, was leased to Amtrak during the first half of the 1970's. The car was stenciled "Leased to NRPC" adjacent to the door below the Southern insignia. (J.W. Swanberg)

Amtrak sleeper 2420 is the only one of its kind on the roster in 1979. The 8 duplex roomette, 6 roomette, 4 double bedroom car is the former Northern Pacific 372, built by Pullman in 1954. The car is shown here in the consist of the Empire Builder departing Minneapolis in October, 1977.

Until the arrival of the Superliners, Amtrak offered only three sleeping car accomodations to the traveling public: the roomette, the bedroom (some were former compartments) and drawing rooms. The latter was offered on the Southwest Limited, Broadway Limited and some of the Florida trains. This photo shows the interior of a bedroom with an annex with complete washroom facilities — note the door to the left of the sofa seat. The lower berth folded down from the wall behind the seat, while the upper berth was lowered from the ceiling. In addition to the sofa seat, a moveable chair was part of the seating in the room. (Amtrak)

Some bedrooms offered sofa seating by day, which turned into a lower berth by night, with the upper berth folding down from the wall, or lowering from the ceiling. An inviting, comfortable way to travel on either overnight trains or all the way across the country. (Amtrak)

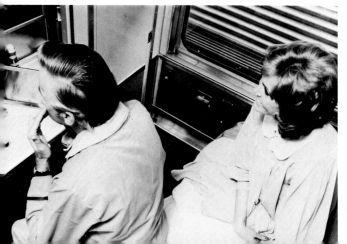

Bedrooms with the long sofa seating sometimes offered a mini-dressing table and combination sink. The toilet was enclosed in an annex. (Amtrak)

Amtrak operates a small fleet of Rail Diesel Cars, mostly in the Northeastern United States. The company has on order self-propelled Amfleet style coaches for service on the Springfield, Mass. line. This RDC-1 and 2 was photographed at New Haven in August, 1975. (J.W. Swanberg)

Still another style of coach and club car service is the "Metroliner". These high speed trains provide 110 miles per hour service between New York and Washington, and literally can beat the airlines at their own game in the Northeast Corridor. (Amtrak)

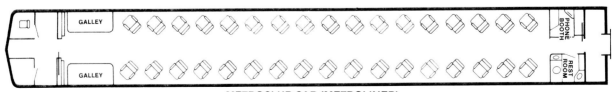

METROCLUB CAR (METROLINER)

Metroclub car seating, until 1979, provided the usual single, reclining, rotating parlor car seat and was highly popular with businessmen. (Amtrak)

A relatively unsung electric service on Amtrak is the 600 series trains between Harrisburg and Philadelphia. Train 440, Washington section of the Broadway, races a Silverliner out of Harrisburg; but it is really no contest since the Silverliner must make frequent stops and 440 can sail right on through. The Silverliners provide 2-3 coach seating for suburban service in eastern Pennsylvania. The photo was taken from 440 in October, 1975. (Patrick C. Dorin).

The United Aircraft Turbos spent a relatively unsuccessful time of operation in the United States, but did provide the concepts for an expanded turbo train service in both the east and mid-western United States. This five car set is operating as train 153, the Yankee Clipper, en route from Boston to New York City over the old New Haven railroad. The train is near New Haven, Connecticut in August, 1975. (J.W. Swanberg)

Amtrak purchased a fleet of Turboliners directly from France, and has operated them on a variety of routes out of Chicago, such as Detroit, St. Louis, Milwaukee and Port Huron. The five car speedsters contain a power-coach at each end, two coaches and a center combination food-beverage and coach car. Some of the cars are equipped with what is called "Custom-Class". Custom Class is arranged in a spacious 2-1 configuration (similar to club car seating) with large reclining seats, upholstered in striking red velour with added legroom and comfortable foot rests. The Custom Class is located adjacent to the Turbo-cafe on those Turboliners so equipped.

This Turboliner is train No. 350 coasting to a stop at Jackson, Michigan en route from Chicago to Detroit in August, 1975. (Patrick C. Dorin).

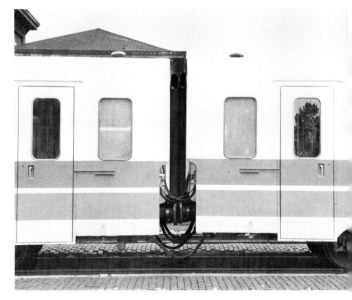

The first set of turboliners went into service complete with European style couplers and buffers. (Patrick C. Dorin).

The French style turboliner coaches are somewhat smaller than U.S. versions, and somewhat lighter in weight. The cars do feature large picture windows and the squared off effect reminds one of the C&NW "400" coach windows. (Patrick C. Dorin).

Amtraks's newest Turboliners represent a blend of American and French designes and engineering and feature larger cars and more space including club car seating on some train sets. The Americanized models, built by Rohr Industries in California, are in service on the Adirondack, DeWitt Clinton, Henry Hudson, Washington Irving, Empire State Express and the Salt City Express on the New York City - Albany - Montreal and Buffalo routings via Conrail (formerly New York Central) and the Delaware and Hudson. This Amtrak photo shows the Rohr built Turboliner on the Department of Transportation test track in Colorado.

The Rohr built models have a capacity of 265 passengers with spacious, comfortable interiors. Food and beverage service is provided from Amfleet style cafe bar centers. The coach seating too is very similar to the Amfleet cars. (Amtrak)

The Amfleet cars are literally the most modern look in U.S. passenger railroading. Built by Budd, they feature the same high standards found in that company's construction for the last 30 years. The cars were originally designed for short distance service only, but have found themselves in many long distance trains, such as the Pioneer and the North Star. (Patrick C. Dorin).

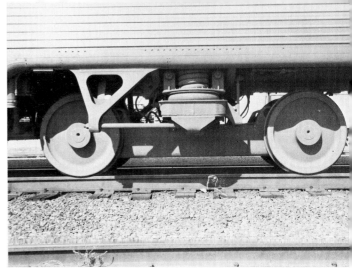

Amfleet passenger car trucks are of a new and unique design, and are quite smooth running. (Patrick C. Dorin).

The cars are 12 feet, 8 inches high; exactly the same height as the orginal Chicago & North Western - Union Pacific "City of Denver" equipment. This measurement, from rail to top of roof, is approximately 10 to 12 inches shorter than conventional streamlined equipment. The curved sides are also similar to other Union Pacific early "City" streamliners built in the 1930's. Consequently the design is not entirely new, but notice the absence of steam lines. Head-end electric power supplies heating and air conditioning needs — a concept pioneered by the C&NW in the late 1950's with the long distance bi-level 400's.

The interiors of the Amfleet are pleasant with soft comfortable seating, carpeting on the floor and walls, indirect lighting as well as direct individual reading lights above each seat. The comfort index is high for both the short distance 84 seat and the 60 leg rest seat cars. (Budd Company photo by Edward H. Johnson, Jr.)

Each Amfleet seat has a full down, fold out, table from the seat ahead. This table does not interfere with the reclining ability of the seat, and provides passengers with a place to eat, play cards, write letters or any other type of activity that can be accomplished on a small table. The tables are ideal for keeping children occupied with coloring books. (Amtrak)

Parlor observation 3770 was often used in parlor car service on the former Amtrak Twin Cities Hiawatha during the early history of the corporation. The car was sold in 1977 and is no longer in Amtrak service.

Amtrak operates two styles of club car accommodations on the Amfleet. the most common is the combination coach-club car with 28 coach seats and 18 club seats separated by the food service bar in the center of the car. The other is the 33 seat club and food service bar car. In both instances, the cars utilize a 2-1 seating with spacious surroundings, carpeting and fold down tables. The seats are larger than the coach chairs and follow what has become the Canadian tradition of 2-1 seating. However, it might be remarked that such seating was available on the Chesapeake and Ohio Railway in "coaches" during the 1930's. As of 1979, travel by Amclub has become the standard for **First Class** daytime travel in the United States. (Amtrak)

Originally Amtrak provided parlor car service on a small number of routes out of Chicago, and on a wider variety of trains in the Northeast Corridor. In 1971, it was the typical "1-1" seating with reclining, rotating chairs. Although interesting to ride, the capacity of such equipment was simply too low for economical operation. This seating arrangement was found in car 3770, the former Great Northern's "Port of Seattle", and contained only 17 seats plus a drawing room for day parlor room service.

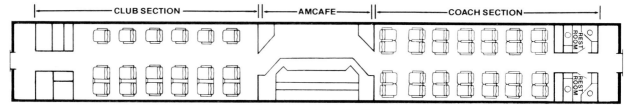

CLUB SECTION — — AMCAFE — — COACH SECTION

REST ROOM

REST ROOM

EXAMPLE OF AMCLUB

The new French-American turbine trains include **First Class** accommodations for the daytime traveler with large, spacious 2-1 seating. Such accommodations have been available on the new turbine trains operating in New York State as well as between New York and Montreal. (Amtrak)

Probably the most unique train on the Amtrak System will be the Canadian built LRC, which stands for **L**ight, **R**apid, **C**omfortable. Amtrak, as of this writing in early 1979, has leased two of the trains for service on the Vancouver, British Columbia - Seattle - Portland route over the Burlington Northern, but have not yet been delivered. The train features a tilting-body suspension system that permits operation around curves faster than normal trains. VIA Rail Canada also has some of these types of trains on order. (Amtrak)

Amtrak has on order 284 bi-level cars from Pullman-Standard, that were to have been delivered and in operation well before the Spring of 1979. The concept for such bi-level long distance operation can be traced to the Chicago & North Western Railway's bi-level 400's, placed in service in 1958 and '59. Eventually purchased by Amtrak, the 96 seat coaches served on a variety of routes out of Chicago. At the present time (1979), the cars are serving in Regional Transportation Authority commuter service in the Chicago area, but were pressed into long distance service during the Christmas, 1978 holiday period. Car 9614 is a full coach. (Patrick C. Dorin and Frank Schnick).

Few will deny that Santa Fe's Hi-level cars were among the best for luxury coach travel in the United States. Actually preceeding the C&NW bi-levels in construction by two years (1956), the cars provided leg rest seating for 72 passengers — 68 passengers in a so-called step down car. The latter was equipped with a stairway at one end of the car with the car diaphragm at standard level to permit operation with conventional cars. Amtrak has operated the hi-level cars on the Sunset Limited, Lone Star and Southwest Limited during recent years. These cars were photographed in the consist of train 16, the Lone Star on the Santa Fe's main line at La Plata, Missouri. (Bob Clark).

The entrance to the Santa Fe Hi-level cars is a little smaller than the door way to the C&NW Bi-level cars. However, the doors on the new Superliners reflect the Santa Fe design. (Bob Clark)

This photo by A. Robert Johnson illustrates a former Santa Fe Hi-level coach, a step down car, coupled to a conventional leg rest coach in train No. 4, the Southwest Limited, at Albuquerque, New Mexico. During the train's stop, a portable washer gives No. 4 a scrub down, getting rid of many miles of desert grime.

Amtrak's Superliner fleet is the latest in American rail passenger car design. As of late 1978, Amtrak had accepted only one coach. The construction and delivery of the new equipment has been plagued by a lengthy strike among other problems. The cars are very similar to the Santa Fe Hi-level cars, and are scheduled to be used on the western routes. Coach 34002 is shown here being rolled out of Pullman-Standard's shop at Hammond, Indiana. (Amtrak)

The Superliner coaches set a new standard for long distance rail travel. In addition to reclining seats with foot and leg rests, the cars feature overhead luggage racks, drinking water fountains, four restrooms and a ladies' lounge equipped with vanity table, chairs, wash basins and mirrors. (Amtrak)

The new Superliner bi-level coaches make long distance travel most comfortable. Built by Pullman-Standard, the equipment can seat 77 passengers with 62 on the upper level and 15 on the lower. Hopefully the cars will be in service by the time this book is in print. (Amtrak)

As with the Amfleet equipment, all seats feature tray tables that lower to provide a flat, stable surface for food and beverages or en route work or relaxation. Each seat has individually controlled reading lights for personal preference. (Amtrak)

The lower level provides seating for 15 passengers and also includes restrooms, ladies' lounge and additional space for storage. The lower level features the same type of seating as the upper level. (Amtrak)

The Superliner coaches are designed to be accessible to the handicapped traveler. Wider aisle and special ramps provide full mobility for wheelchairs. The special seats recline, swivel and have folding armrests so that a handicapped passenger can easily transfer to or from their wheelchairs. Specially equipped restrooms are located nearby. (Amtrak)

Superliner coach 34013 is equipped with 77 leg rest seats for long distance luxury travel. The new bi-level cars carry some unusual lettering that was once customary on many roads, particularly the Union Pacific and Southern Pacific. For example, the car type (in this case "COACH") is indicated at the car ends (in the lower stripe) and in big bold lettering adjacent to the entrance. The SP continued this practice until recent times. The 34013 was photographed at the Santa Fe coach yards in Chicago on February 3, 1979. (Patrick C. Dorin).

The Superliners have also prompted the return of still another custom, the "Road Name" in the letter board. Amtrak can be easily seen in the upper candy stripe. Even more important is the former custom by some roads, such as the UP, SP, C&NW, and Milwaukee Road, of painting the train's symbol-name on the side of the car. The reader may recall the words, "Streamliner" and "Challenger" on the sides of UP and C&NW equipment, not to mention "Daylight" on the SP. Amtrak has revived the custom by splashing "Superliner" on the new bi-levels. Simply fantastic! It adds a note of pride that has been found wanting on the Nation's railroads for at least twenty years. (Patrick C. Dorin).

This photo illustrates the differences between the new bi-level and Amfleet equipment. Obviously the cars could never be coupled together, but they function in much the same way. Electrical power from the locomotive provides constant heating, air-conditioning and other requirements. Consequently steam lines are conspicuously absent, while electrical cables are very much in evidence. Another characteristic is the built in marker lamps showing only red to the rear. The diaphragms of the two types of cars are similar. Although there are no plans at the present, perhaps some Superliners will be converted to step down cars (such as some former Santa Fe El Capitan equipment) so that they can be operated with conventional sized equipment.

When this picture was taken in February, 1979, Chicago was simply overwhelmed by snow. (Patrick C. Dorin).

The new Superliner sleeping cars feature economy rooms, delux bedrooms, family room and special room. The delux rooms feature both sofa and chair seating by day, and two full beds by night as well as enclosed washroom facilities. This is an artist's concept of the bedroom. (Amtrak)

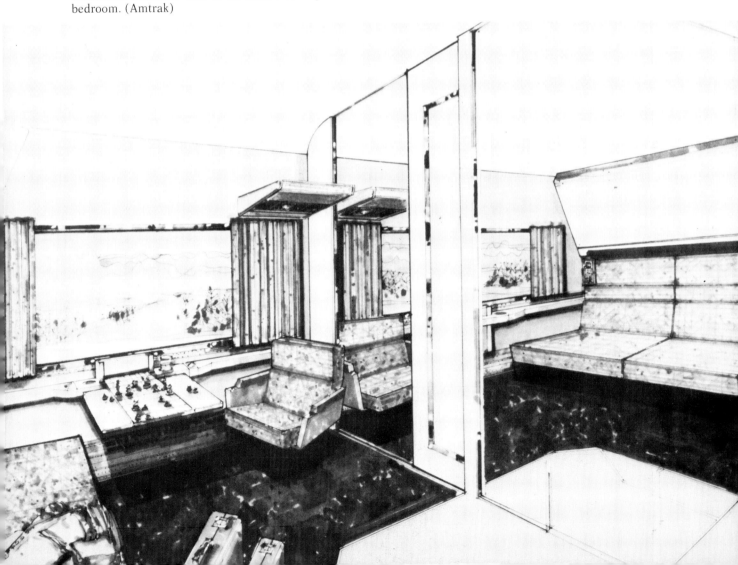

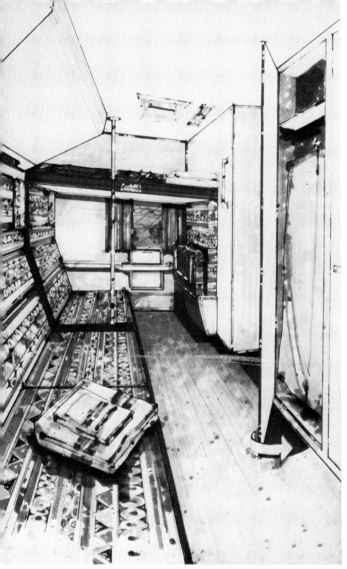

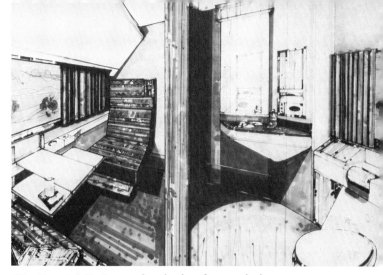

The Special Bedroom for the handicapped also occupies the entire width of the sleeper on the lower level, similar to the family room. The bedroom provides accommodations for two passengers and adequate space for a person in a wheelchair to maneuver.

Hopefully the new Superliner bi-level sleepers, with a capacity of 44 passengers, will be in operation by the Fall of 1979. (Amtrak)

The Family Room is on the lower level and occupies the entire width of the car. It provides sleeping for three adults and one child. (Amtrak)

As of February, 1979, Amtrak is leasing Southern Railway coaches for New York - New Orleans service. (Southern Railway)

Southern Railway sleeping cars were of the highest quality and are now in Amtrak service. This inviting photo shows a Southern sleeping car porter putting the finishing touches on the lower berth in a bedroom. (Southern Railway)

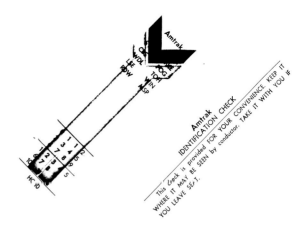

The Southern Crescent was also assigned a dome parlor car between Atlanta and New Orleans. The car once operated on the Wabash Railroad's famous "Blue Bird". (Southern Railway)

Amtrak Identification Checks are punched by conductors to indicate destination of coach passengers. This particular ticket is from the Milwaukee Road section of Amtrak indicating stops between Chicago and Minneapolis-St. Paul.

Amtrak owns and operates five Amfleet/Turbo buffer cars, 10600 to 10604, such as the 10601 shown here — a former Santa Fe coach. The equipment is operated without diaphragms for the purpose of moving Amfleet and Turbo cars from one location to another in conventional trains. This car was photographed at St. Paul in January, 1979. (Patrick C. Dorin).

Amtrak owns one business car, known as Track Inspection Car No. 10000. The author was unable to secure a photo of the car. However, business cars do operate on Amtrak trains rather extensively. For example, Southern Pacific car SP 106, the Oregon, is a frequent traveler on various SP operated Amtrak trains. In addition, the SP 106 is painted Amtrak colors under an old rule that all railroad owned cars must be painted "Amtrak" in order to operate on Amtrak trains. The rule has now been discontinued, and some rail lines have elected to adopt their own color scheme for their own equipment. (Patrick C. Dorin).

CHAPTER 5

Meal and Beverage Cars
and Service

As Amtrak moves through its eighth year, it has standardized its meal service into three basic components: complete dining service, light meals and snack service.

The first is no longer the most prevalent on Amtrak trains in 1979 but it most closely resembles the full meal service of the pre-Amtrak days. Served in full dining cars (or combination dining lounge, diner-coach, etc.), full course meals with all the trimmings, superb linens and so forth are still part of the tradition, and the meals are tasty and the call for dinner in the diner is as inviting as it ever was.

Amtrak originally standardized its menu nationwide. This has reduced both losses and waste in the dining cars, a problem that plagued the railroad industry ever since the depression. The dining car losses, by the way, were a major contributing factor in the overall passenger deficit, and Amtrak has made some wise decisions with dining car service.

Light meals are served in snack bar cars or lounge cars. Light meals include not only sandwiches, but grilled hamburgers, other hot meals and soups. Perhaps not as elegant as dining car meals, but no one need go hungry and the prices are quite reasonable.

Snacks are served either in lounge cars or snack bars and consist of beverages, sandwiches, potato chips and similar items.

Beverage service consists of soft drinks in all food and beverage service cars as well as coffee. Beer and other alcoholic beverages are served in lounge and recreation cars, as well as parlor or club cars. Such beverages are also available to dining car patrons.

The decor of the equipment is done up in bright and cheerful surroundings, with the exception of night club cars, which are done up in typical subdued light, night club atmospheres. A number of U.S. Army hospital cars have been rebuilt by Amtrak for club car service on such trains as the Broadway Limited and others.

Dining and lounge car services are available in all types of equipment including the traditional dining car, hi-level and bi-level dining cars, Turbos and Turboliners, Amcafe cars, combination diner lounges, full lounge cars (including night club and recreation cars), bi-level and hi-level lounge cars and dome lounge cars; including the standard short "Budd" dome as well as Southern Pacific's ¾ length dome lounges, Burlington Northern's Empire Builder dome lounges and Milwaukee Road Super Domes. The equipment is a pleasant way to travel, and the time spent in such only adds to the restfulness of train travel.

Although Amtrak meals have been standardized to a great degree, there are many variations and special orders that can be found throughout the system. For example, Amtrak can supply a variety of kosher meals to its passengers in any part of the country if given 24 hours notice.

Harold Kabel, Amtrak's Chief of Food and Beverage Planning, stated that kosher lunches and dinners are available featuring beef jardiniere, roast boneless breast of chicken and filet of sole almondine. Breakfasts offer either a Spanish or Nova Scotia salmon omelette. Passengers need only specify their preference when making reservations. The packaged meal is served to passengers with the rabbinical seal unbroken and includes kosher eating utensils. Passengers requiring salt-free, low cholosterol or other special diets can consult with the steward on the train's dining car. Food generally can be cooked to a special request, for example without seasoning or butter, or broiled instead of fried.

Many long distance trains carry a supply of food suitable for babies, but Kabel suggests that parents bring their baby's own brand of food along. Baby foods and bottles can be heated in the galley for passengers.

At the present time, Amtrak changes its long haul dining car menus twice yearly to reflect seasonal passenger preferences. This also permits taking advantage of raw food price fluctuations—fresh products are usually cheaper during the summer months and some products are only available then.

Each long haul menu features some "standard" items such as hamburgers, steaks and chefs salads. In addition there are dishes that reflect regional preferences.

Amtrak has geared its menus to the tastes of its passengers—both on items and price. Recent menu changes have tended toward more basic foods that

Nothing could be finer than dinner in the diner in the tradition of the past century of time. The white jacketed waiter serves a couple a meal that was cooked to perfection in the kitchen. The table includes the linen, silverware and even the flowers that have been common place in dining cars on the finest trains. Such tradition has lived on with Amtrak on the long distance trains. (Amtrak)

EXAMPLE OF DINING CAR

Amtrak dining cars can be divided into three basic styles: (1) complete self-contained cars with both kitchen and dining room, (2) a twin unit kitchen and dining room cars and (3) hi-level or bi-level cars with the upper floor containing the dining room, with the lower floor accommodating the kitchen and pantry.

Dining car 8067 is a former Great Northern car originally built for the Empire Builder, and shown here in Amtrak service on the North Coast Hiawatha in December, 1976 at Billings, Montana.

have universal appeal, such as southern fried chicken and roast beef. The thrust has been to increase quality while eliminating expensive items that appeal only to a small portion of passengers.

Linens, tableware and fresh flowers are still part of Amtrak's dining service making dinner in the diner a memorable occasion.

To alleviate the dinner time crunch, Amtrak promoted an "early dinner" served in dining cars between 4 and 5:45 PM. The menu offered a choice of two entrees at a special lower price. Prices in 1979 ranged from $4.75 for filet of sole to $6.95 for complete meals.

There are two types of Amfleet food and beverage cars. The most prominent is the Amcafe car. Actually a combination coach with a food and beverage bar located in the center of the car, the Amcafe is a very sound advancement over the food bar coaches that operated on some railroads prior to Amtrak. This equipment has been nearly phased out as the Amfleet equipment takes over more and more runs nationwide.

The Amcafe is equipped to serve small hot meals, sandwiches, a variety of desserts and beverages, light breakfasts and lunches or just a plain cup of coffee if that is what the passenger desires. The serving bar can be staffed by one or two people and includes electric refrigerators, heating ovens, sink and ice storage.

The Amdinette care is actually an Amcafe with the addition of an adjacent dining room containing eight tables with a seating capacity of 32 people. The passenger has the option of taking his food or drink back to his regular seat in the train, with its drop-down tray, or staying in the Amdinette to socialize with fellow passengers.

The Amdinette car (as well as Amcafe) are operated in both short and, in several cases, long dis-

In addition to the linens and other table settings, Amtrak provides a placemat complete with logo and the greeting, "Nice to have you with us."

tance trains. They are decorated in brown and beige and include carpeting on the floors, walls and ceilings for sound absorption. Baggage racks were not installed in the lounge sections to provide a more spacious appearance. The tables are separated by heavy transparent divider panels. Amdinettes are operated in sit down meal service on the Panama and Montrealer.

The Amfleet cafe and lounge car service provides a very inexpensive and enjoyable source for food and beverages for the wide variety of "Amfleet" train services.

The 35 new bi-level dining cars feature many improvement especially in the kitchen. The new kitchens are all-electric and, naturally, air conditioned. Gone are the "presto" logs with their overpowering heat.

Bi-level dining car kitchens are located on the lower level and have both microwave and convection ovens. Two small elevators raise the food to the upper level where it is served to passengers in fine dining car tradition.

Modern electric refrigerators are used eliminating the need for ice (either dry or wet) except for cold beverages. A unique feature is that the kitchen equipment is removable so that if a unit becomes inoperative it can be pulled out and replaced quickly with a working unit.

Food service provisioning consists of products already pre-portioned and ready for cooking. With this procedure, more types of entrees can be offered without creating an increase in kitchen workload.

Components of the meals are assembled in a central facility, packed in large containers and delivered to the train. Onboard, the chef uses the convection oven to heat the food and then portions it out as orders come in from various waiters.

The bi-level dining cars are full service diners and continue to be the china and linen operation of the past 75 years.

The new bi-level lounge cars are equally efficient. On the lower level is a food and beverage area using a unit similar to the ones on the Amcafe cars. Upstairs is a "wet" bar staffed by an attendant and comfortable swivel chairs for passenger "see-level" viewing convenience.

A trip to the dining and/or lounge car makes a trip that much more enjoyable.

Former Seaboard Coast Line diners featured a novel arrangement of tables and seating for dining car patrons. (Bob Clark)

Interior views of former NP dining car looking toward car entrance and toward the kitchen. (Patrick C. Dorin and Bob Clark).

Amtrak diner 8047 was the former Northern Pacific 461, and has the distinction of being part of a group of dining cars that were to be the last constructed until the Superliners in 1979. The Budd Company built the diners for the NP and CB&Q in 1957. The car is serving in train 8, the Empire Builder, at Minneapolis in 1976.

Hi-level dining car 9984, from the former Santa Fe's El Capitan, introduced an entirely new concept in train travel dining. With the kitchen on the lower deck, the car is able to seat 80 passengers at one time in the full length dining room on the upper level. Amtrak 9984 is shown here operating in the Southwest Limited at Winslow, Arizona. (A. Robert Johnson)

Amtrak 8101 is a combination lunch counter diner and comes from the Santa Fe, the former 1556 built by Budd in 1948. Linens and flowers are not part of this equipment's fare for it (and other cars like it) serve sandwichs, snacks and beverages on long haul trains (such as the Coast Starlight) and for short distance (such as the Blue Water, Arrowhead and the Puget Sound before Amfleeting) operations nationwide. The 8101 was photographed between runs at Seattle in March, 1975. (Patrick C. Dorin).

Still another example of lunch counter equipment is the 8340, the former Union Pacific 5008 built by St. Louis car in 1959 for the "City" streamliners. Photographed in February, 1975, the car was assigned to east coast trains at that time. (J.W. Swanberg)

A step down from the lunch counter cars were the coach-snack bars, such as Amtrak 3957, the former New York Central 3091. The snack bar coaches operated on a variety of short distance trains, such as the Empire Service out of New York City. The menu included sandwiches, beverages and something for one's sweet tooth, but generally could not serve hot meals as could be obtained on the lunch counter cars. Nevertheless, the snack bars were (and are) an excellent addition to an otherwise short distance coach train. This car is serving on train 74, the Water Level Express at Harmon, New York in February, 1975. (J.W. Swanberg)

One of Amtrak's many problems was the wide variety of equipment from the various railroads. This snack bar coach was originally a "400" coach from the Chicago & North Western, which had been sold to the Great Northern. The GN blocked out one window in the smoking compartment, and turned it into a buffet, which was used to serve passengers on the Gopher and Badger trains. Amtrak later leased the car from the Burlington Northern and operated it on the Arrowhead between Minneapolis and Duluth, the very same route of the former Great Northern twins mentioned above. The car is in service on the Arrowhead in this October, 1975 photo. (Patrick C. Dorin).

There were many combination sleeper-diner, or sleeper-lounge or diner-coaches, and even coach lounges built for the railroads over a 50 year period ending about 1960. One such car was the combination sleeper-diner lounge, City of Cleveland (and running mate City of Chicago) for the Nickel Plate Road. Amtrak served light meals and beverages on the cars, which operated on such runs as Chicago - Washington. The car was photographed in train 40 at Harrisburg, Pennsylvania in October, 1975. (Patrick C. Dorin).

Another example of Amtrak combination cars was the 9250, the Wawasee, a former B&O 5 double bedroom, buffet lounge car originally built for the C&O. Wawasee was operating mid-train in Florida service when this photograph was taken in September, 1973. (J.W. Swanberg)

The interior decor of such combination equipment was usually simple, functional and cheerful. The triangular tables made dining a little more unusual than the customary style found in dining cars. The interior shown here is the former Great Northern coach-diner originally constructed for the International between Seattle and Vancouver. (Patrick C. Dorin).

Six double bedroom lounge car, Amtrak 3222 - Palm Beach, carried an experimental color scheme with a solid blue stripe through the window area. For this reason the car is historically significant. (J.W. Swanberg)

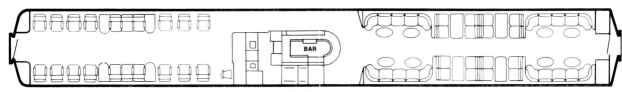

EXAMPLE OF LOUNGE CAR

Amtrak has operated a number of Observation lounge cars, but in almost all cases, the cars operated mid-train for beverage service to both coach and sleeping car passengers. Such equipment also served sandwiches and snacks, and took on quite an atmosphere during the late evening hours. Tavern Lounge Observation car 3335 is being switched into the consist of train 11, the Coast Starlight, at Seattle in September, 1973. (J.W. Swanberg)

Of the lounge cars, the domes were highly favored and Amtrak operated three types: full length, the short dome and the SP's home made ¾ length, "every seat under glass" domes. Of the full length, there were two types: the Milwaukee Road's Super Domes and Burlington Northern's Great Domes. The latter operated almost exclusively in the Empire Builder and the North Coast Hiawatha, and provided the usual menu of sandwiches, snacks and your favorite beverage. This former BN Great Dome, the 9362, and its sisters have seen a variety of service not only on the transcontinentals, but also on passenger specials for the Governor of Minnesota and Director's Specials on the Great Northern, and later the Burlington Northern, and Duluth, Missabe & Iron Range Railway. The 9362 is serving in the consist of train 8 departing Minneapolis on a foggy day in August, 1976. (Patrick C. Dorin).

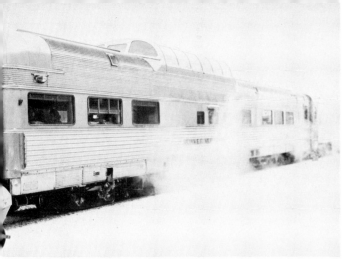

When the Great Domes were in the shops, a Budd short dome often substituted, such as the Silver Veranda, a former Dome Observation Parlor car from the Burlington. Refitted for snack and beverage service, the car is serving mid-train on train 8 at Havre, Montana, in March, 1975, during a cold stinging, biting snow storm. (Patrick C. Dorin).

Short Domes were more common on the North Coast, such as Silver Lounge (a combination dome lounge, buffet, dormitory car) in the consist of old No. 9 (later renumbered 17) at Billings, Montana in December, 1976. (Patrick C. Dorin).

Not all Amtrak dome observations were squared off, such as the 9310, a former Wabash Blue Bird car. Converted for lounge car service, the car is operating in coach service for ski train, Extra 538 West pausing at Cambridge, Minnesota en route from Duluth to Minneapolis in December, 1977. (Patrick C. Dorin).

Two of the former Denver Zephyr dome "Chuck-Wagon" cars were refurbished with a touch of the "Old West". Designed in warm copper tones, the rebuilt cars featured copper formica counters, rust tweed carpeting, walls done in a barn board for a weathered, rustic effect and denim upholstery. The dining-lounge room provided seating for 23 people while the lunch counter offered eight seats. As usual there were 24 dome lounge seats plus a dormitory area for the dining and lounge car crews. These dome cars were among the most interesting designs of interior decor created by Amtrak. (Amtrak photos)

UPPER LEVEL

LOWER LEVEL

Amtrak refurbished the SP domes in pleasant colors that were restful to the eye, such as oranges and browns. This photo shows the lower lounge as well as the stairway to the upper level, and demonstrates the "every seat under glass" SP advertising. (Amtrak)

Still another Amtrak creation was the "Discodome", a lively rolling cabaret car which enabled passengers to mix fun and scenery. The "Discodome" was patterned after the successful bistro car, which had been so popular on the Canadian National's Rapido trains between Montreal and Toronto. The "Discodome" featured a downstairs piano with lounge seating for 15 people as well as hot and cold light meal service. Upstairs in the dome passengers could relax at a series of quad tables. The walls of the "Discodome" were also carpeted. (Amtrak)

A favorite dome of many travelers was the Southern Pacific's ¾ length dome lounge. The equipment has served primarily on the San Francisco Zephyr and the Coast Starlight, two trains that travel over the SP's Overland, Shasta and Coast Routes.

The former SP dome lounge provides table seating adjacent to the serving bar in the lower level. A dining car attendant is walking through the car signaling meal time with the traditional chimes. (Amtrak)

The refurbished seating in the SP cars feature circular and serpentine sofas. (Amtrak)

Amcafe-coaches represent the latest design in combination coach food bar cars with a substantial improvement, particularly in the menus offered. Complete meals as well as snacks and beverages can be secured from the center of car serving area. Note the windowless area on car 20015, a 56 seat coach-cafe car. The car is en route from the Budd Company to Seattle for Pacific Northwest train service in the summer of 1976. (Patrick C. Dorin).

Food Service cars carry sub-lettering in the corners as well as designations, such as "Amcafe", and Amdinette". (Patrick C. Dorin).

Food and beverages are loaded on the Amdinette of train 21, the Inter-American at Chicago's newly remodeled coach yards at 12th Street. (Patrick C. Dorin).

Amdinettes feature table seating where passengers may take their meals, served on an attractive tray, to eat and enjoy the company of fellow passengers. Amdinettes can seat 32 passengers in the dining room. On some trains, such as the Montrealer and Panama Limited, table linens and flowers are part of the decor as well as sit down meal service with waiters in the traditional concept of dining car service. Amcafe-coaches, or Amcafe-club cars do not contain the dining room section as can be seen in this photo. (Amtrak)

The central service area of the Amfleet (as well as the Metroliners) feature a serving bar, coffee makers, refrigerators, micro-wave ovens and scores of cabinets and drawers for food storage, trays and eating utensils. Service is generally quite fast, and passengers interviewed by this writer indicated that they are quite pleased with this type of food service arrangement. (Amtrak)

The Amfleet's fold down tables at coach and club car seats allow passengers to enjoy their meals at their own seats. (Amtrak)

The interior decor is based on the Indian art of the Southwest Indians. It was hoped that equipment assigned to the Empire Builder and North Coast Hiawatha would have featured Northwest Indian art, but as of this writing, such is not to be the case. The serving area for snacks and beverages is on the lower level of these fantastic Superliner cars. (Amtrak)

Club car passengers are served meals by the attendant, from the central serving area of the Amclub or combination Amclub-coach-cafe car. (Amtrak)

Meal preparation and assembly area of the Superliner kitchen. (Amtrak)

The Rohr Turboliners, with the blend of American and French designs are also equipped with Amfleet style food service centers. Minus the curved walls of the Amfleet equipment, the Turboliners give a feeling of a bit more space in the serving area. (Amtrak)

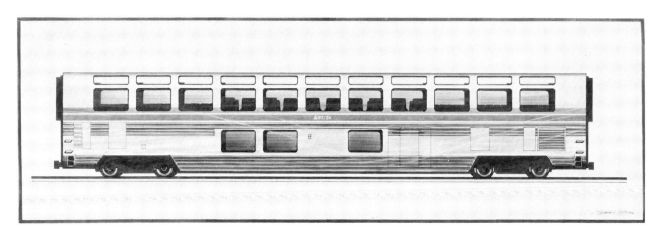

(Above) Amtrak's new bi-level Sightseer/Lounge car will afford excellent visibility from its many large windows. (Below) Diagrams of lower and upper levels show possible seating arrangements in the new cars.

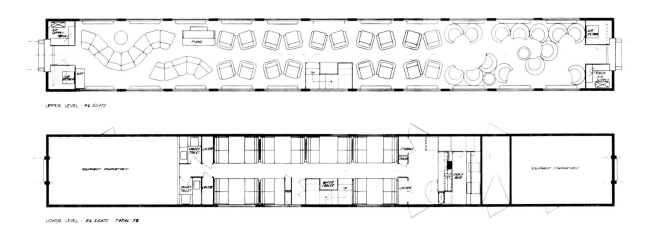

UPPER LEVEL · 46 SEATS

LOWER LEVEL · 26 SEATS   TOTAL · 72

Amtrak's new bi-level lounge cars for the transcontinental trains are similar in many ways to the Santa Fe hi-level lounge cars. The equipment contains table seating on both levels and, for extra visibility, 27 inch windows curving into the roof line. (Amtrak)

During the summer of 1971, Amtrak leased Santa Fe Big Dome lounge cars for service on the Texas Chief. Santa Fe No. 512 was eventually sold to Auto-Train and was converted to a "Dome Night Club" car for their Florida service. The car is shown here departing Chicago on the former Texas Chief, later renamed the Lone Star. (Patrick C. Dorin).

As of February, 1979, Amtrak is operating Southern Railway dining cars in the Southern Crescent through a lease-purchase agreement. This interior photo illustrates Southern Railway dining car decor and hospitality. (Southern Railway)

The Superliner dining cars also follow a similar pattern of the former Santa Fe hi-level equipment. The dining room is on the top level, while the kitchen, pantry and other mechanical equipment is located on the lower level. (Amtrak)

Amtrak provides very attractive napkins for meals and snacks aboard dining, lounge, cafe and dinette cars. (Patrick C. Dorin).

Southern Railway is also providing a sleeper buffet lounge car for the Southern Crescent. The interior decor is regarded as one of the finest to be found in such equipment throughout North America, and was actually a drawing card for passengers traveling on the Southern again, and again. The car also contains a Master Bedroom, sleeping facilities for three adults complete with shower facilities; and a drawing room, also with two lowers and one upper berth. With Southern dining and lounge car services, an entirely new dimension has been added to Amtrak food and beverage services. (Southern Railway)

Chapter 6

Mail and Express Traffic

Traditionally head-end traffic has consisted of mail, baggage, express and milk, and it has been carried in passenger type equipment with large doors and generally without windows; although a number of these cars were constructed with one or two windows for different reasons. For example, some Milwaukee Road baggage cars contained a window at the rear of the car for a conductor's office, a practice seldom found on any other railroad. Baggage cars have included not only the passenger car type, but also box cars and refrigerator cars equipped with high speed trucks and train and steam lines for passenger service.

The other type of head-end car is known as the Rail Post Office car. This car carried mail clerks who sorted the mail en route from one location to another. The RPO was equipped with windows for the benefit of the clerks who needed to be able to tell the location of the train.

For the most part, Amtrak owns a fleet of baggage cars from the Santa Fe, Penn Central, Union Pacific and a number of other lines plus the United States Army. There are a few variations with most the cars being 70 to 85 feet long with two doors on each side. The U.S. Army cars are about 50 feet long with but one door on each side. There are some combination baggage coaches, baggage buffet lounge cars, baggage parlor and baggage dormitory cars.

Amtrak also owned 8 Rail Post Office cars which were operated in the Northeast Corridor on special mail trains operated for the U.S. Postal service only. This RPO service was discontinued in 1977.

As Amtrak began operation, it used baggage cars for passenger luggage and for a very small amount of mail. Indeed, it was almost non-existent, for the postal service had been on a drive to place all mail on trucks or planes, even though they admitted it would cost more.

However, it did not take long for the postal service to recognize that Amtrak trains might be very advantageous for mail transportation. Mail revenue began to move up. In 1971 Amtrak earned $ 1.2 million in operating revenues. By 1973, mail revenue increased to $ 4.4 million. A large part of this was due to the establishment of mail service on the Chicago — Los Angeles route as well as a general increase in volume on the already established mail operations.

In early 1974, a joint program had been undertaken by Amtrak with the U.S. Postal Service to improve the handling of mail and to reduce the overall workload through containerization of mail in baggage cars. Evidently the joint program worked because mail revenues rose to $ 6.2 million in 1974 and showed a further gain to $7.3 million in 1975 and $ 7.6 million in 1976 and $ 10.5 million in 1977.

Further increases in mail traffic are taking place on a number of routes, and the situation is much more encouraging that it has been for many years. Some postal people have privately admitted that it was a mistake for the RPO cars to be taken off as they were during the 1960's. Perhaps we will see their return on Amtrak routes throughout the U.S.A.

Nearly everyone recalls the Railway Express Agency, or as it was more recently known, REA Express. The former name could be found on baggage cars of every railroad that participated in the Express service. That company is now totally out of business, but prior to its folding up completely in the mid-1970's, it had given up operating over the railroads even though there were some novel techniques, for example mini-containers on 85 foot flats that could slide on or off at terminals and intermediate stations. There were a variety of reasons for the eventual folding of the organization but one of them was the over pricing of the service. The demand for the type of service is well illustrated by the success of United Parcel Service, which by the way, ships a great deal of its traffic "piggyback".

Two F-40PH's with a steam generator car set out one leased Southern Pacific baggage car of mail en route from Chicago to the Twin Cities at the new Midway Station on the west side of St. Paul. The car traveled in train 7 from the Post Office in Chicago and is loaded with containers. The mail cars are unloaded, and then reloaded and returned to Chicago on train 8 the following day. The date of this photo is July 25, 1978. (Patrick C. Dorin).

Prior to the leasing and expanded useage of the SP cars, Amtrak leased a number of streamlined Northern Pacific streamlined baggage cars from the Burlington Northern. This March, 1975 photo shows mail being loaded and unloaded during a rather severe snow storm in Havre, Montana. Train 8, the Empire Builder, is but two hours off the time card despite the storm. Trains 7 and 8 handle a substantial amount of mail across the route of a very famous mail train, Great Northern's 27 and 28; and fortunately the mail traffic is continuing to improve over this route between Chicago and Seattle. (Patrick C. Dorin).

Amtrak has operated a variety of baggage cars since 1971, including such cars as former Great Northern baggage-dormitory No. 1203, now renumbered and repainted Amtrak 1553. This particular car contained a 30 foot baggage compartment and a sleeping capacity for 23 crewmen. These former Great Northern cars continued to operate in such trains as the Empire Builder until the bi-level equipment was phased in during 1979. This car is in the consist of train 8 rounding the curve into the Chicago Union Station during the summer of 1972. The absence of additional baggage cars reflect the lack of mail and express business during the early days of Amtrak. (Patrick C. Dorin).

It is the summer of 1976, and the Empire Builder is carrying an additional baggage car for mail and express, instead of just simply a baggage dorm. During the mid-1970's, Amtrak began to actively seek additional mail and express traffic, and it slowly but surely began to pay off. This former Santa Fe baggage car was and is typical of the head-end cars operated on many Amtrak trains from Coast to Coast. The Minneapolis post office can be seen in the background gleaming in the early morning, Minnesota "Sun Rise". (Patrick C. Dorin).

Amtrak baggage car 1377 is a former United States Army Kitchen car rebuilt for mail car service. Such equipment was not only rebuilt for conventional service, but by 1977 several were rebuilt for operation in Amfleet trains. The 1377 is in the consist of the Arrowhead en route from Duluth to Minneapolis handling a newly acquired mail contract between the Twin Ports and the Twin Cities. The car is shown at Cambridge, Minnesota. (Patrick C. Dorin).

With the demise of REA, and the recognition of the demand for such service, Amtrak placed into service a low cost rail package express service on July 1, 1973 between major cities across the nation. There were three special express services known as priority, economy and custom. The establishment of the new service complied with the 1972 amendments to the Rail Passenger Service Act of 1970, which provided that the Corporation must take actions to increase its revenues from the carriage of mail and express. Thus an entirely new concept in passenger train express service was introduced. The rates and charges were designed to take advantage of Amtrak's unique ability to establish a new form of cargo transportation unencumbered by the technical regulations and complex rate structures previously "inflicted" upon the railroads by the various governmental regulatory agencies.

As mentioned previously, Amtrak offers three special express services. The first is Amtrak Priority Package Express. It is a high-speed, small package service between Washington and New York.

The shipments must be under 25 pounds each and move on a priority basis on Amtrak's high speed trains, the Metroliners. There is a flat charge of $ 10.00 between any two points. Shippers are instructed to have the packages at the Amtrak express office 30 minutes before train departure. Shipments are available for pickup at destination approximately 30 minutes after the train's arrival. The shipments are easily identifiable as Priority Express because they are carried in special red, white and blue Amtrak bags.

Amtrak Economy Package Express covers normal, express type traffic between 280 cities on Amtrak's system that are served by trains carrying

Baggage car 1035 is former Santa Fe 3519, and is one of the cars modified in the interior for the transportation of mail containers, and electric operation in Amfleet trains. The car is shown here in the consist of train 8 in mail service at Minneapolis in August, 1976. (Patrick C. Dorin).

through baggage/express cars. The rates are per the hundred weight depending upon distance. A minimum rate of $7.50 is charged.

The maximum weight per piece is 75 pounds, and the maximum weight per shipment is 350 pounds, unless advance arrangements are made for larger shipments. Economy Express shipments should be brought to the originating station at least one hour before departure, and is available for pickup at the destination one hour after train arrival. Train baggage masters sort the shipments en route and see that the express is expedited to station forces.

Amtrak Custom Express is an individualized, specialized service to accommodate frequent, regular express uses. The services and rates, also to 280 cities, is tailor made depending on the service requirements and characteristics of the traffic. Space is reserved in express cars for this kind of shipment, which includes such items as publications,

drugs and pharmaceuticals, automotive parts and other items too numerous to mention here.

An extensive public information and ad program was carried out to acquaint the public with the express service. It was reported that there was a gain of 26% in express revenue in 1977 over 1976 and that the service, which began in mid-1973, brought in $ 120,727 the first year, and has grown to over $ 2.2 million in 1977. Amtrak predicted further gains in their express and mail traffic revenue in 1979, and has been remodeling baggage cars to be compatible with both the new Amfleet as well as the older conventional equipment.

The baggage car has been traditionally the car one would find behind the locomotive and ahead of the coaches in a train. However, it is not unusual to find such equipment on the rear end of trains for easy set out at intermediate terminals. Such traffic is proving to be very beneficial to Amtrak, and it will bear watching over the next few years.

Baggage-dormitory 1502, named San Simon, was originally constructed for the Santa Fe's Chief in 1937. The car was photographed in the consist of train 11 at Seattle in December, 1976. (Patrick C. Dorin).

Southern Pacific 6710 represents still another variety of leased SP baggage cars, this one with a different style roof. The car was photographed at the mail loading track in Minneapolis in 1977. (Patrick C. Dorin).

Amtrak baggage 1001 is a handsome 85 foot car, formerly CB&Q No. 902, the Silver Express, constructed by the Budd Company in 1940. The car still retains its skirting and has had over 38 years of continuous service. Photographed in 1977 at Minneapolis in mail service. (Patrick C. Dorin).

Not all head-end traffic operates on the "head-end". This Southern Pacific baggage car was added to the Empire Builder at Minneapolis, and the most convenient placement was behind the sleeping cars. On this February, 1978 winter day, the Empire Builder, train No. 8, is running as train 10 because it is over 12 hours late. At the time this photo was taken, trains 7 and 8 ran overnight between Chicago and the Twin Cities, while trains 9 and 10 provided day service. After April, 1978, the situation was reversed with 9 and 10 running on the overnight schedule between Chicago and Duluth via St. Paul. This photo shows the Builder departing Wisconsin Dells over the Milwaukee Road's Second Subdivision of the Wisconsin Division in double track, automatic block signal territory. (Patrick C. Dorin).

Baggage car 1266 has been modified for operation in trains with both steam lines as well as electrical operation. Such equipment can travel system wide in both conventional and Amfleet trains. The car is en route to Duluth as part of the consist of the North Star during the summer of 1978. (Patrick C. Dorin).

One of the unusual head-end cars operated by Amtrak is car 9995, part of a fleet of six baggage-dormitory cars with Hi-level adapters for the former Hi-level El Capitan, now known as the Southwest Limited. The car was photographed in the consist of the "Limited" at Winslow, Arizona on the Santa Fe on May 2, 1976 by A. Robert Johnson.

The mail loading track at the St. Paul "Midway" Station in 1979 sees more and more business as time goes on. The capacity of the track is five cars, and when additional cars must be loaded or unloaded, they frequently occupy one of the through station tracks. With the recent increases in the mail and express business, perhaps this scene will repeat itself more often throughout the Amtrak System. (Patrick C. Dorin).

At small stations, such as LaPlata, Missouri on the Santa Fe, it is a relatively easy and quick task to throw aboard a sack of mail and a half dozen suitcases being checked through to Chicago on train 16, the Lone Star. (Bob Clark)

At large depots, the task of loading mail can be quite simple provided the Post Office uses containers. Simply back up a Postal semi-trailer and roll the containers out of the truck and into the baggage car. Unloading is equally efficient. (Patrick C. Dorin).

A variety of types of containers are used by the U.S. Postal Service and Amtrak. This older model looks more like a cage, and consists of two separate sections. The tag on the container indicates all mail on the right hand side is destined to the state of Washington, while that on the left is going to Oregon. This photo shows mail that had just been loaded on a baggage car on train 5, the San Francisco Zephyr, at Denver, Colorado on December 24, 1978. (Patrick C. Dorin).

The U.S. Postal Service places a placard for destination on each rail car or truck that is loaded with mail. This card indicates that Amtrak baggage car 1002 is traveling from Denver, Colorado to Chicago with 70 feet of mail pay length with "preferential" U.S. Mail on December 24, 1978. (Patrick C. Dorin).

During the Christmas mail rush of 1978, Amtrak not only continued to borrow Southern Pacific baggage cars, but also went to Burlington Northern for at least one car. The 7025, which is sometimes used as a baggage-recreation car on BN special trains, was loaded with mail for western destinations at St. Paul, Minnesota. (Patrick C. Dorin).

The D&H was simply not content with D&H equipment and a leased CP dome, but operated the train with Alco "PA's". Train 68 is preparing to depart the CP's Montreal depot on August, 1974 with 3 coaches and a dome coffee shop coach carrying the markers. (J.W. Swanberg)

Chapter 7

Amtrak Trains in Action

Amtrak has operated a variety of trains throughout the United States and Canada, not only from a historical point of view, but also from a geographical and equipment point of view. To begin with, trains operated with rolling stock and motive power from the member railroads. As time went on, motive power and passenger cars were repainted in the Amtrak color schemes. A complete photo album would be required to show the entire transition, a task that must still be completed for the railroad history library.

It is frequently commented that with all equipment painted Amtrak, and the advent of the Amfleet and Superliners, that all Amtrak trains are the same. Nothing could be further from the truth. Depending upon assignment, terminals, population densities, mail contracts and even express traffic; Amtrak trains vary quite widely. Serving different clientel, trains vary in length, type and style. The book has already discussed some of the interior configurations. It is the purpose of this chapter to illustrate the wide variety of trains operated and the purpose for which they were operated. Amtrak is definitely not the same all over, and the differences will become more obvious as time goes on.

Train 40, the Broadway Limited, departs the Chicago Union Station for New York and Washington, D.C. with 4 "E" units and 16 cars tied to the drawbar of the last diesel. The Broadway Limited operates over the former Pennsylvania Railroad as of this writing, but changes may be in store with the January, 1979 Department of Transportation recommendations. See the Epilogue. (Amtrak)

BROADWAY LIMITED

Another view of train 40; this time arriving at Gary, Indiana with 18 cars and powered by four Penn Central "E" units. In these January, 1973 photos, the Broadway is the only transportation going east as a freezing rain is falling. The train has a full load (many of them air line passengers) and has a former B&O observation lounge sleeper from the Capitol Limited carrying the markers. (Patrick C. Dorin).

Of all the Amtrak trains the Adirondack, between New York and Montreal, looked the least like an Amtrak train. The Delaware and Hudson prefered to operate trains 68 and 69 with home owned equipment and motive power plus a leased Canadian Pacific dome coffee shop coach. Aside from the ticket one held, it was difficult to tell if it was Amtrak or D&H service. The leased CP dome was perfect for the upstate New York scenery. At the time of this writing (1979), passengers no longer have the option of domeliner service with a Turboliner doing the honors.

(Delaware and Husdon Railway Photo by Richard Allen, Courtesy of Amtrak)

Harrisburg, Pennsylvania — just the name brings many fond memories for many travelers. Pennsy K-4's traded places with the immortal electric GG-1's for the final leg to New York City. However, in 1979 the romance is not gone. Trains 40 and 41 split or combine with 440 and 441 respectively, the Washington section. Diesels must trade with electrics, and GG-1's still do the honors. Consequently, at least 30 minutes is consumed with switching and motive power changes. This photo shows train 40 at the Harrisburg depot early in the morning in July, 1976. (Bob Clark)

An extremely popular train is the Lake Shore Limited between New York and Chicago over the former New York Central trackage of Conrail. Train 49 is clipping along the three track main line with 11 cars by the mighty Hudson River on June 30, 1978. No. 49 will pick up the Boston section at Albany and will be even longer for its overnight run to the Windy City. (J.W. Swanberg)

During 1975, trains 440 and 441 operated between Harrisburg and Washington via the Columbia and Port Deposit branch line along side the Susquehanna River. After 1975, the trains ran via Philadelphia. The writer rode train 440 on a dark and rainy day in Octover, 1975, and this photo shows the GG-1 rounding a curve with the four car train. Note the welded rail along side the track. (Patrick C. Dorin).

Lake Shore Limited

NATIONAL LIMITED

The National Limited provides service between New York, Washington, Pittsburgh, St. Louis and Kansas City. Once called the Spirit of St. Louis, trains 30 and 31 have had more than their share of troubles— much of it because of extremely poor Penn Central trackage. This photo shows train 30, with new SDP-40-F's, departing Pittsburgh with 8 cars over former PC trackage. Almost five years after this photo was taken, trains 30 and 31 are powered by F-40-PH's and are equipped with Amfleet cars. Furthermore, the 1979 schedule would not permit train 30 to have its photo taken in the same location as it passes through Pittsburgh in the dark. (Amtrak)

It is the year 1973 and train 75, the Empire Service, arrives at Croton, New York with Penn Central E-8, No. 262, leading six cars on its afternoon run from New York to Syracuse. (J.W. Swanberg)

In October, 1973, train 71 was a daylight run from New York to Buffalo. According to the time table, 71 offered checked baggage, coach, snack and beverage service. Obviously the latter was offered in observation car 3341, the former Seaboard 6601, built by Budd in 1947. (J.W. Swanberg)

Another view of train 75, this time at Ossining, New York in electrified territory behind Penn Central P2B, No. 4626. This October, 1973 version has but three cars for its run to Syracuse. Train 75 was eventually named the Washington Irving. (J.W. Swanberg)

The date is May 5, 1974, and train 74 with 9 cars races along the Hudson on its daylight dash from Buffalo to New York. Rail photographer J.W. Swanberg caught the train on film at Peekskill, New York. The reader may note the different shade of color on the last three coaches. Three MTA commuter coachers are providing overflow space for Amtrak was short of equipment. Commuter coaches from New York, Boston and other eastern cities frequently provide extra seats for passengers during heavy travel periods throughout the eastern section of the U.S.A.

Electric power was, and is, required for trains originating or terminating in New York City. Consequently, former New York Central P2b's provide road power for Amtrak trains between New York and Croton-Harmon. Penn Central No. 462 is moving train 74 with four cars by Ossining, New York in the four mainline track electrified territory (third rail), during its fast run from Buffalo to New York City in May, 1974. (J.W. Swanberg)

By 1975, the name Empire Service for the New York State trains was dropped in favor of individual train names. Additional trains were placed on the schedule too. Things were definitely looking up for the former New York Central main line. Train 62, in 1975, was called the Salt City Express, and provided a morning 5 hour, 50 minute schedule between Syracuse and New York City. With E-8 No. 216 doing the honors, the five car train is arriving at Peekskill, New York on May 23, 1975. (J.W. Swanberg)

Except for the Niagara Rainbow, which is equipped with Amfleet cars, the entire New York State service on the Conrail and the Delaware and Hudson railroads is provided with Turboliners. The Adirondack, Dewitt Clinton Henry Hudson, Washington Irving, Empire State Express and Salt City Express look just like this train, which was constructed by Rohr Industries. The only other train through the New York State corridor is the Lake Shore Limited, and that train is equipped with conventional rolling stock. (Amtrak)

What was once an Amtrak daytime run between New York and Pittsburgh, the Duquesne, train No. 25, arrives at Lancaster, Pennsylvania with a PC GG-1 and three coaches. One of the former roomette cars on the head-end had been modified by the Penn Central to include a snack bar. The GG-1 and the rails are gleaming with droplets of water on this misty, April, 1972 afternoon. (Patrick C. Dorin).

Train 70, the Henry Hudson, glides toward New York on Conrail trackage during its fast morning run from Albany. The Turboliners are equipped with special electrical pickup shoes for the third rail operation between Croton-Harmon and New York City. (Amtrak)

GG-1's looked equally well on either short or long passenger trains, such as No. 174, the Statesman charging through New Haven, Connecticut on April 4, 1974. The rear nine coaches are borrowed commuter cars for the heavey week-end travel. (J.W. Swanberg)

The Metroliners have been serving the New York - Washington territory for nearly 10 years as of this writing. They represent America's fastest trains, but have never been able to fully operate at the 160 miles per hour once projected. Nevertheless, the Metroliner is one of the best ways to travel between the Nation's Capitol and Manhattan. With the newly reconstructed track in the Northeast Corridor, the Metroliners may soon be able to show even greater potential. (Amtrak)

Still another phase of Amtrak service is the Silverliners, the 600 series trains between Philadelphia and Harrisburg. This westbound Silverliner is arriving at Harrisburg after its 107 minute run for the 103 miles from Philly over the former Pennsy mainline, now Amtrak. (Bob Clark)

This photo demonstrates just how busy the Northeast Corridor can be. From left to right, one can see an electrified commuter train en route to Connecticut points, a Conrail Alco RS-3, No. 5520 powering a work extra; while on the far right Amtrak E60, the 960 rolls the Minute Man around both trains near Stamford, Connecticut on Amtrak trackage. (J.W. Swanberg)

This particular scene has become prevalent on Amtrak's Northeast Corridor as the new electrics power equally new Amfleet cars on a variety of trains between Washington and Boston. At the time of this writing, electric power must be exchanged with diesel locomotives at New Haven, but plans include electrification from that point to Boston. (Amtrak)

East of New Haven, at the time of this writing, diesel electrics power the Amfleet cars. This particular train is eastbound on Amtrak Railway trackage and is passing the marina at Mystic, Connecticut. (Amtrak)

The Florida trains: before and after Amtrak the train between New York and Florida has been one of the best ways to travel to fun in the sunshine. Always long, the GG-1's were up to handling the 18 to 20 car long trains with ease. Penn Central 902 picks up speed on train 86, the Champion, departing Washington for the final leg of the Florida - New York City journey. The date is September 10, 1973. (J.W. Swanberg)

It is early in the morning on December 29, 1977 and train 93, the Miami section of the Floridian, is being assembled at the Jacksonville, Florida depot. The Floridian served the Chicago - Florida market traveling over the L&N and SCL railroads. (Bob Clark)

The Silver Meteor, a former Seaboard New York - Florida train, is framed by the palmettos on its run through the Florida "Gold Coast" near Hollywood. Amtrak has continued the fine tradition of Florida train travel on the New York runs. However, the Floridian on the Chicago run has been hurt substantially because of poor trackage. The potential of the Chicago - Florida run has yet to be even scratched; and the Detroit - Florida traffic has yet to be even considered. Although the January, 1979 DOT Report recommends discontinuing the Floridian, a better option would be to revise schedules and re-routing over better trackage. (Amtrak photo by Ira H. Wexler)

Floridian

Since May 1, 1971, Amtrak operated the Southern Crescent north of Washington, D.C. Here the 4896 threads through crossovers at the New Rocelle, New York tower with train 172, the Southern Cresent, on November 18, 1974. (J.W. Swanberg)

South of Washington, the Southern Railway operated the Southern Crescent until February 1, 1979. This photo shows the train No. 2 passing the Jefferson Memorial en route to Washington Union Station and Amtrak trackage to New York. The reader will note that the Southern diesel bears a giant decal of Thomas Jefferson, which it wore as part of Southern Railway's salute to the Bicentennial. There was a decal for each of Southern's passenger engines, honoring one of the signers of the Declaration of Independence from each of the states Southern serves. (Southern Railway)

The green and gold paint of Southern Railway's Southern Crescent flashes in the morning sun as the train pulls into the Alexandria, Virginia depot. For the first few months, the Southern Crescent will retain its Southern Railway look as the cars and locomotives will be leased instead of purchased outright. There is no doubt about it, the Southern Railway had an ideal color scheme, and operated a very fine train. (Southern Railway)

Southern Railway train No. 1, the Southern Crescent, has just arrived in Atlanta and passengers are departing the depot after having a restful overnight journey from Washington, D.C. The Southern Railway is to be commended for its fine service to the traveling public. (Southern Railway)

.

Amtrak posed the "Blue Ridge" at Harpers Ferry, the sight for many Baltimore & Ohio Railroad publicity photographs. The Blue Ridge provides daily service between Washington, D.C. and Martinsburg, West Virginia. It is essentially a long distance commuter train providing morning service to Washington, and evening service to West Virginia. (Amtrak)

Amtrak train 50, the Cardinal, strolls along the Baltimore and Ohio's Akron-Chicago Division main line in north west Indiana during its run from Chicago to Washington. At Wellsboro, Indiana, the train will turn off the B&O and on to the Chesapeake and Ohio for the remainder of the run to the East Coast. The consist of the train includes the General Electric P 30, the 712, two baggage cars, one 10 roomette-6 double bedroom sleeper, one Amfleet dinette-coach and three Amfleet coaches. (Frank Schnick and Patrick C. Dorin).

The **Shenandoah operates** between Washington and Cincinatti over the Baltimore and Ohio. This photo shows train 33 rounding a curve as it enters Oakland, Maryland, westbound for points in West Virginia and Ohio. (Amtrak)

The **Chicago - Detroit trains** were downgraded substantially by the Penn Central. In fact, prior to May 1, 1971, they had been downgraded to two trains each way as simple two car scoots—although scoot they did not. After May 1st, the trains were immediately upgraded by Amtrak, and patronage began to climb. And this was happening in the Motor State! This photo of train 362, the St. Clair, on September 11, 1973, departing Chicago for Detroit shows part of the growth. Five and six car trains were becoming common over the old Michigan Central route, and it was indeed refreshing. (J.W. Swanberg)

Eventually trains were added to the route between Chicago and Detroit. One such train was the Michigan Executive. Basically a commuter train, the Exec provides service from Jackson to Detroit in the morning, and from the Motor City in the evening. This photo shows train 374 at Jackson in the very early morning in August, 1975. (Patrick C. Dorin).

The Jackson, Michigan train board has not seen this many trains listed since the New York Central days. The photo was taken in August, 1975.

The Executive was advertised throughout Southeastern Michigan, and one could find signs such as this one in the Jackson depot in various areas. The Michigan Executive was the result of action by Michigan citizens and the State government. (Patrick C. Dorin).

Another new Michigan train was the Blue Water Limited, between Chicago and Port Huron. The train literally operates over three different railroads between terminals: Conrail, Chicago to Porter, Indiana; Amtrak, Porter to Kalamazoo; Conrail to Battle Creek and the Grand Trunk Western Railway, Battle Creek to Port Huron. In this photo, train 64 (Amtrak No. 364) is traveling in excess of 70 miles per hour just west of Lansing during its run to Port Huron. (Patrick C. Dorin).

As of 1979, the Blue Water Limited is equipped with a French built Turboliner. Grand Trunk Western first class train No. 65 pauses at the East Lansing, Michigan depot for passengers during the summer of 1978. It might be remarked that the Grand Trunk's tracks are among the best in the U.S.A. (Patrick C. Dorin).

Train 351, The Wolverine, en route from Detroit, threads its way through the puzzle switches at the entrance to the Chicago Union Station on May 25, 1975. (J.W. Swanberg)

Bob Clark captured on film train 351 on a dark snowy/rainy day in Battle Creek prior to the re-equipping of the Detroit trains with Amfleet equipment. As of 1979, all three sets of trains, the Wolverine, Saint Clair and the Twilight Limited are Amfleet and include club car service. As a result of the Turboliners and later the Amfleet cars, patronage continues to climb on the Michigan runs, and second section running is not infrequent on heavy travel week-ends.

This view of train 351 was taken from the rear-end of train 374 at the West Detroit tower on what is now Conrail trackage in August, 1975. (Patrick C. Dorin).

Amtrak train 355, the Twilight Limited en route from Detroit to Chicago, glides along Amtrak trackage in automatic block signal territory near the Indiana-Michigan border in September, 1975. (Paul Stringham)

In the days before Amfleet, Amtrak photographed
one of the Chicago - St. Louis trains on the Illinois
Central Gulf (the former Gulf, Mobile and Ohio Railroad). Note the Baltimore and Ohio style signals, re-
flecting that company's influence on the old Chicago
and Alton of days long gone by. (Amtrak)

Train 350, the Wolverine, arrives at Kalamazoo, Michigan on Amtrak rails with Detroit bound passengers. Since 1977, Amfleet has been standard equipment on all of the Detroit trains offering coach, cafe and club car service. (Bob Clark)

Train 331, the morning Turbo from Chicago to Milwaukee pauses at Sturtevant during its 92 minute run over the Milwaukee Road. (A. Robert Johnson)

On a bright and cheerful Sunday morning in August, 1975, Amtrak train 763, the Arrowhead sails by a strawberry patch during its morning run from Duluth to Minneapolis. The route is the former Great Northern trackage, now the BN's First Subdivision of the Wisconsin Division. The photo was taken a few miles north of Cambridge, Minnesota.

The Arrowhead probably saw more types of equipment and a wider variety of motive power than any other Amtrak System train. At one time, Amtrak leased DM&IR passenger SD-9's and they handled the five and six car trains with ease. Train 766 is approaching Cambridge with five cars on its run to Duluth in March, 1977. (Patrick C. Dorin).

Originally the Arrowhead was scheduled to run to the Twin Cities in the morning, and to the Twin Ports of Duluth-Superior in the evening. Patronage sagged badly, and so, the schedule was reversed and traffic soared beyond one's wildest immagination. This photo shows train 761 arriving at Superior (from Duluth) in June, 1977 shortly after the change in the train's schedule. The Arrowhead is on Lake Superior Terminal and Transfer Railway trackage and to the right is the main freight yard of the company. (Patrick C. Dorin).

As of April, 1978, the Arrowhead was technically discontinued between Duluth and Minneapolis. It was replaced by a new train, the North Star—a Chicago - Duluth run via the Twin Cities. This photo of train 9, running as 760, pausing at Cambridge, Minnesota shows the typical consist of one baggage car, one 10 roomette-6 double bedroom sleeper, one dinette-coach, one 84 seat coach and one 60 seat leg rest coach. Patronage sometimes requires as much as four more Amfleet cars for loadings in excess of 400 passengers. The North Star has been a very popular train, and the finest way to travel between Duluth-Superior and Chicago. (Michael Dorin)

Train 10, the North Star, en route from Duluth to Chicago pauses to load substantial mail, unload and load passengers and for servicing at St. Paul on February 2, 1979. (Patrick C. Dorin).

Train 9, the Twin Cities Hiawatha, approaches the Wisconsin Dells, Wisconsin depot on February 17, 1978. With two coaches, coach-dinette and two baggage cars on the rear, the Amfleet train is the smoothest run over the Milwaukee Road since the Hiawatha coaches of yesteryear. As of April, 1978, The Twin Cities Hi was replaced by the North Star on an overnight schedule retaining the train numbers 9 and 10. The overnight schedule of the "Star" is very close to that of the Milwaukee Road's "Pioneer Limited" between St. Paul and Chicago. Day service between Chicago and St. Paul is currently (1979) provided by trains 7 and 8, either the Empire Builder or North Coast Hiawatha. (Patrick C. Dorin).

A favorite set of equipment of the author's was the former C&NW bi-level 400 equipment. The cars have served in various capacities on a number of Amtrak runs out of Chicago, such as the Illinois Zephyr. This photo shows train 348 headed by E-unit No. 288 during its run from Quincy to Chicago at Mendota, Illinois on July 2, 1975. (Paul Stringham)

The IZ can be quite crowded on week-ends and during holiday periods. Paul Stringham photographed the Zephyr with four bi-levels at 79 miles per hour with General Electric P30CH No. 710 providing the locomotion. Eastbound 348 is traveling over the Second Subdivision of the Burlington Northern's Chicago Division in CTC territory with both tracks signaled for operation in both directions.

The Empire Builder was once the pride of the former Great Northern fleet, and continued to be a popular train after the BN merger and Amtrak. Since May 1, 1971, the Builder has traveled over Milwaukee Road rails between St. Paul and Chicago. This photo shows former 32 (now 8) during its LaCrosse, Wisconsin station stop for passengers and water for the aging F-7's on the head-end. The time is June, 1972 and the Builder carried former NP slumbercoaches and a diner and Great Dome in the BN color scheme. (Thomas Dorin)

EMPIRE BUILDER

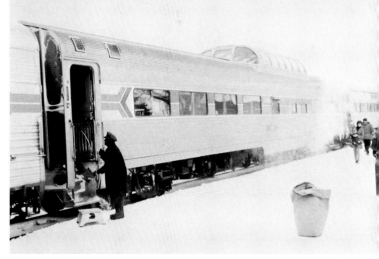

The North Coast Hiawatha provides train service between Chicago and Seattle via the southern Montana route over the former Northern Pacific. A populous and important routing, the train services several Montana and North Dakota cities as well as the Yellowstone National Park through Livingston, Montana connections. The former No. 9 is pausing at Billings, Montana for servicing on the BN's Second Subdivision of the Yellowstone Division on December 9, 1976. (Patrick C. Dorin).

During recent winters Montana and North Dakota have had some rather severe snow storms. Indeed as of this writing on February 16, 1979, all highways and expressways from western Minnesota to eastern Montana are blocked with snow and no highway travel is possible. Indeed air travel, too, has been suspended. Although the trains are running late, Burlington Northern is still operating the Amtrak services, which says something of the dependability of train travel. This photo by Michael Dorin was taken during a severe snow storm with wind driven ice crystals at Havre, Montana. The Empire Builder, train 8, is about two hours late in this March, 1975 photo and the porter is trying in vain to clean out the vestibule.

Train 5, the San Francisco Zephyr, departs Chicago for its run to Oakland, California on a beautiful, sunny afternoon in September, 1973. The 14 car train consists of mostly former Burlington equipment, and the train reminds one of the California and/or Denver Zephyrs. The Chicago - California train operates over the Burlington Northern, Union Pacific and Southern Pacific railroads. (J.W. Swanberg)

The Panama Limited, between Chicago and New Orleans, over the former Illinois Central (Now Illinois Central Gulf) provides overnight service between the Great Lakes and the Gulf of Mexico. This June, 1975 photo shows the train with conventional streamlined equipment with SDP-40F's for power. During 1977 the train was equipped with Amfleet cars and still later with a sleeper converted for operation with such equipment. Dining service is no longer the type offered by the once proud IC, but sit down dining complete with table cloths and table settings is provided in the Amdinette. This photo shows train 58 departing New Orleans for Chicago. Although a fine train, the orange and brown is sadly missed by many along the Illinois Central (Gulf). (J.W. Swanberg)

THE PANAMA LIMITED

At least through December, 1978, SDP-40F's provided the power for the long distance San Francisco Zephyr. This photo by Paul Stringham shows train 6 coming to a gentle halt next to the Burlington "Hudson" No. 3006 at the Galesburg depot. The 3006 had a much longer service history than Amtrak's 622 and its running mate will ever have. Perhaps, at least one SDP-40F should be preserved for the sake of history.

Train 6 arrives at Chicago with 16 cars in May, 1976. (J.W. Swanberg)

During train 5's run to the West Coast, locomotives are changed at Denver, Colorado. Furthermore, since the train travels from Denver to Cheyenne, Wyoming, No. 5 heads into the Denver depot in a southerly direction. The fresh locomotive couples on to the rear-end of the train and pulls it backwards for the 107 miles to Cheyenne. At Cheyenne, the locomotive reverses ends and pulls the train forward again on its westward journey over the Wyoming Division. This photo shows the 621 and 586 coupled on to the rear of No. 5 at Denver, which incidently will run as Extra 621 West over the Union Pacific. Another interesting point of trivia is that the UP allows passenger trains 90 miles per hour running over certain segments of the Wyoming Division, while some types of freights are allowed 70. The Union Pacific is to be commended for its excellent track. (Patrick C. Dorin).

The two SDP-40's have changed ends, and unit 628 will lead (after trailing from Denver) train 5 from Cheyenne to Oakland on April 25, 1976. (A Robert Johnson).

This photo shows the head-end of train No. 5 at Denver on December 24, 1978. With the reverse running to Cheyenne, these baggage cars are actually the rear-end of Extra 621 West. (Patrick C. Dorin).

Southern Pacific/Amtrak train 5, the Zephyr, pauses to change crews and service the train at Sparks, Nevada on the Sacramento Division on December 25, 1978. (Patrick C. Dorin).

During the early days of Amtrak, the Southern Pacific assigned four FP-7 diesel units to the Zephyr. No. 5 is shown here paralleling the Truckee River near Reno, Nevada. The ten car train is not unlike the consist of the "City of San Francisco" minus, of course, the Rail Post Office car and an additional mail storage car. However, the "City" could and did swell to 18 to 20 car consists during the summers and holiday travel periods.

It should be mentioned that the SP between Reno and Oakland is also the route of the Reno Fun train. This winter season train, operated on week-ends, has been highly successful not only for Amtrak, but also the SP before May, 1971. The train has turned into a tradition for Northern Californians. (Amtrak)

Train No. 5 rounds a curve in the Sierra Nevadas on Christmas Day, 1978 on the Roseville Subdivision of the Sacramento Division in Automatic Block Signal Territory. (Patrick C. Dorin).

The Pioneer began service in June, 1977 between Salt Lake City and Portland - Seattle. Originally, the train was equipped with a simple Amfleet consist of a coach-dinette and two or three coaches. By 1978, the train also carried a 10 roomette, 6 double bedroom sleeper and a baggage car. The train operates as 25 and 26 between terminals, and makes direct connections with 5 and 6 respectively at Ogden, Utah. The writer feels that 25 and 26 should be utilized to carry through Chicago - Portland cars in connection with the Zephyr.

The Pioneer travels over the Union Pacific between Salt Lake City and Portland and the Burlington Northern between Portland and Seattle. Additional coaches are added at Portland westbound, and set out on the eastbound trip. The Pioneer is the only train service over what was once the "City of Portland" route of the UP. (Amtrak)

SOUTHWEST LIMITED

One of Amtrak's most cooperative railroads is the
Santa Fe. This photo shows train 4 arriving in Chicago
from Los Angeles, and once was called the Super Chief.
Now renamed the Southwest Limited, the train retains
much of the charm of the AT&SF. The Hi-level chair
cars of the former El Capitan, as well as the sleepers,
lounge and dining cars provide first class service as
well as bringing back fond memories of Santa Fe tra-
vel.There seems to be fewer problems on Santa Fe
trackage than on other lines. Perhpas it might be the
warmer climate. (J.W. Swanberg)

Flagstaff, Arizona, is an important stop for trains 3 and 4, the Southwest Limited. Located on the Third District of Albuquerque Division, the Santa Fe maintains two main tracks, a Train Control System (Santa Fe jargon for Centralized Traffic Control) and Automatic Train Stop. Much of the District is authorized for 90 miles per hour. This photo shows train 4 pausing for passengers on May 2, 1976. (A. Robert Johnson).

Santa Fe-Amtrak train 4, the Southwest Limited, barrels along at nearly 90 miles per hour on the high speed main line near Galesburg, Illinois. The big SDP-40F's have not been placed under a variety of speed restrictions on the Santa Fe as on other railroads. It is probably a credit to Santa Fe trackage. (Paul Strigham).

Santa Fe-Amtrak train No. 4 is serviced during its Winslow, Airzona stop. The Southwest Limited regularly draws three SDP-40F's, and is one of the few trains to do so on a regular basis. Winslow is located on the east end of the Second District of the Albuquerque Division. The entire Second District, Gallup to Winslow, has a maximum authorized speed limit of 90 miles per hour for passenger trains. (A. Robert Johnson).

The Santa Fe operates one other long distance Amtrak train, the Lone Star between Chicago and Fort Worth-Dallas, and Houston. The train operates on a fast schedule, and was formerly named the Texas Chief. This photo shows train 16 departing LaPlata, Missouri with former Santa Fe Hi-level coaches and a Pine series sleeper carrying the red mars light. The train is picking up speed quite fast during the early twilight of a new day as it rolls towards its Windy City destination. (Bob Clark)

SUNSET LIMITED

Another train that was assigned former Santa Fe Hi-Level cars was the Sunset Limited, trains 1 and 2, between New Orleans and Los Angeles over the Southern Pacific. This photo shows the Sunset Limited traveling across the southwestern desert on the Tucson Division.(Amtrak)

As of early 1979, the Santa Fe operates six Amtrak trains in each direction between Los Angeles and San Diego. Not since the mid-1950's have so many trains graced the Third and Fourth Districts of the Los Angeles Division. Furthermore, most of the Fourth District is equipped with Automatic Train Stop as well as Train Control System (known as TCS). Consequently, passenger trains are authorized for 90 miles per hour between Sorrento and Santa Ana. Most of the trains, collectively known as the **San Diegans** are equipped with Amfleet equipment, such as this train at Los Angeles Union Station. (Amtrak)

The San Diegans

The Coast Starlight between Los Angeles and Seattle over the Southern Pacific and Burlington Northern railroads has proven to be an immensely popular train. In the early years the SP assigned FP-7's and SDP-45's, which were later replaced by Amtrak's own SDP-40F's. This photo shows train 13, en route from Los Angeles, traveling along the Santa Barbara Subdivision of the Los Angeles Division in the early morning fog near Ventura, California. The consist of the train, a whopping 18 cars, not unusual at all for the Coast Starlight. (Amtrak)

The Coast Starlight

Train 14, the Coast Starlight, eases around the mainline curve at Pryer, Oregon on the Cascade Subdivision of the Oregon Division; as a BROAF (running as Extra 8467 West) moves slowly through the CTC controlled siding. For those freight train symbol enthusiasts, BROAF stands for BRooklyn yard (Portland), OAkland Freight. Train 14 met and passed several freights between Klamath Falls and Eugene, Oregon during the author's trip on December 27, 1978.

Passenger service to and from Amtrak trains at San Jose, California is provided by Southern Pacific commute trains on the San Francisco Subdivision of the Western Division. The SP provides excellent connections with modern double deck and standard coaches, all of which are exceptionally clean and painted a rich dark grey. Train 120 is shown here at the San Francisco depot on December 26, 1978.

Despite the shortage of equipment, Amtrak has operated many passenger extras during its eight year history. During the summer of 1971, the company sent a Turbo on a National tour to acquaint the public with the new style train. This photo shows the Turbo rolling into the Galesburg, Illinois depot on September 4, 1971 with a huge crowd to greet it. It brought back memories of when the original Burlington Zephyr rolled through Galesburg on both exhibition runs and its famous dawn to dusk run from Denver to Chicago. The Turbo, however, showed that people still turn out to see a train. And it makes the writer wonder why so many of the railroad companies sell themselves short! (Paul Stringham)

The consist of train 14 on December 27, 1978 was a grand total of 19 cars, the longest Amtrak passenger train ridden by the author. Included in the consist were two baggage cars, ten coaches, three food and beverage cars, including a former SP dome lounge and a diner coffee shop of Santa Fe heritage, three sleepers and finally a SP business car, the 106 - the Oregon. Train 14 is shown here during its Eugene, Oregon stop with the brakeman on the ground complying with Rule 99, otherwise known as the rear-end flagman rule.

The patronage of the train was heavy enough to warrant the entire consist. The business car was set out at Portland and the remaining 18 cars completed the trip over BN trackage to Seattle.

Another extra, again with a Turbo, was operated through New York state to campaign for State Transportation Bond issue. The date, October 31, 1973, was almost symbolic. The irony being that the failing Turbo was used to promote the bond issue. The Turbos are, as of this writing, out of service and their future is at best uncertain. (J.W. Swanberg)

Even President Ford used a train to campaign. This photo shows Amtrak's track inspection car, No. 10000 on the rear end of a passenger extra consisting of Amfleet equipment whistle stopping at Durand, Michigan — on the super track of the Grand Trunk Western Railroad. (David J. Balzer)

When equipment must be moved from one part of the system to another, it either moves in regular trains or as an extra. When the Amfleet went west to Southern California and to the Pacific Northwet, it went in a solid consist as a special movement. This photo shows the San Diegan equipment en route to Los Angeles on the Santa Fe in 1976.(Amtrak)

Amtrak ran a "Ski Train" on a series of Fridays in late 1977 and early 1978 between Minneapolis and Duluth. On those days, the regular run went North in the morning. Then the train returned to the Twin Cities as an Extra shortly after noon. At 6:00 p.m. the equipment made still another run to Duluth, returning later in the evening to Minneapolis. One set of equipment made two round trips. The regular southbound schedule out of Duluth was annulled on the Friday operation of the ski train. This photo shows the southbound extra that had departed Duluth at 1:25 p.m. stopping at Cambridge.

762	760	◄——Train Number——►	761	763	765
The Arrowhead		◄——Train Name——►	The Arrowhead		
Friday Only thru Mar. 24	Daily	◄ Frequency of Operation►	Ex Fr thru Mar. 24, then Daily	Friday Only thru March 24	
⊖ 🏛	⊖ 🏛	◄——Type of Service——►	⊖ 🏛	⊖ 🏛	⊖ 🏛
6 00 p	8 30 a	Dp......ST. PAUL/......Ar MINNEAPOLIS, MN	9 05 p	5 00 p	2 30 a
E 7 15 p	E 9 45 a	.......Cambridge ●........	E 7 48 p	E 3 43 p	E 1 13 a
E 8 00 p	E10 30 a	......Sandstone, MN ●.....	E 7 00 p	E 2 55 p	E12 25 a
9 25 p	11 55 a	........Superior, WI.......	5 50 p	1 45 p	11 15 p
9 45 p	12 15 p	Ar.....DULUTH, MN.....Dp	5 30 p	1 25 p	10 55 p

How does Amtrak schedule a passenger extra for the traveling public? In some cases, a special time table is issued for the traveler's information. This schedule shows the timing for the ski specials, which were even given train numbers—Amtrak train numbers that is. However, the trains (except for the regular run 760) ran as extras. The train order shows how the train was scheduled on the First Subdivision of the Wisconsin Division as an extra. Boylston is located just south of Superior, Wisconsin, while Coon Creek is just west of Minneapolis. Between Duluth and Boylston and Coon Creek and Minneapolis, the trains ran on other subdivisions, and similar orders applied on those very short distances. (Amtrak and Burlington Northern)

Amtrak passenger trains are not the only passenger trains to operate over Amtrak Railroad lines between Washington and Boston. New Jersey commuter service between Trenton and New York adds to the wide variety of train traffic in the Northeast Corridor. This eastbound "Jersey Arrow" is slowing for Colonia, New Jersey with a four car consist. (Harold Zabel)

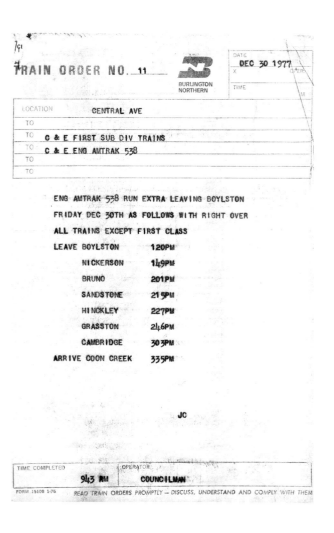

TRAIN ORDER NO. 11

BURLINGTON NORTHERN

DATE DEC 30 1977

LOCATION	CENTRAL AVE
TO	
TO	C & E FIRST SUB DIV TRAINS
TO	C & E ENG AMTRAK 538
TO	
TO	

ENG AMTRAK 538 RUN EXTRA LEAVING BOYLSTON
FRIDAY DEC 30TH AS FOLLOWS WITH RIGHT OVER
ALL TRAINS EXCEPT FIRST CLASS

LEAVE BOYLSTON	120PM
NICKERSON	149PM
BRUNO	201PM
SANDSTONE	215PM
HINCKLEY	227PM
GRASSTON	246PM
CAMBRIDGE	303PM
ARRIVE COON CREEK	335PM

JC

TIME COMPLETED	OPERATOR
943 RM	COUNCILMAN

FORM 15108 1-76   READ TRAIN ORDERS PROMPTLY — DISCUSS, UNDERSTAND AND COMPLY WITH THEM

Passengers detrain at Chicago's Union Station from a
Superliner equipped train. The new bi-level cars are the
newest Amtrak equipment in late 1979. (Amtrak)

Amtrak's new Superliner coaches went into service for the first time on February 26, 1979, operating between Chicago and Milwaukee, Wisconsin. The two coaches, 34013 and 34014 were powered by F40PH locomotive No. 230 and operated out of Chicago for a few weeks on various short runs to familiarize on-board services and operating crews with the new equipment.

(Photo for Amtrak by J. David Ingles, TRAINS Magazine)

Chapter 8

Amtrak Freight
and Work Equipment

With the Penn Central failure, Consolidated Rail Corporation took over substantial amounts of trackage of not only the PC, but also the Erie-Lackawanna, Reading and Central of New Jersey. Amtrak purchased several segments, such as those sections from Porter, Indiana to Kalamazoo, Michigan; Harrisburg, Pennsylvania and Washington, D.C. to Boston, and New Haven to Springfield, Mass. Most of the equipment is used for track work and the massive reconstruction projects now underway on Amtrak owned lines. Amtrak is truly now its own railroad, with its own crews, motive power, equipment and dispatchers. ConRail has trackage rights over all Amtrak lines.

Con Rail itself has fallen on difficult times, and in this writer's opinion, the organization is unmanageable because of the wide variety of traffic patterns throughout the system. Consequently car control is nearly impossible. (During an interview with a traffic manager of a Twin Cities firm by this writer it was stated that ConRail consistently looses carloads of raw materials en route from New Jersey to Minneapolis. Therefore, the company has requested shipment by truck, even though it is more costly. Burlington Northern too loses out even though it is not at fault. This is mentioned here because ConRail problems affect Amtrak.) Because of this, there is a possibility that ConRail will be broken up into smaller, more manageable companies. Amtrak could conceivably take over some of the freight services, in this writer's opinion.

However, it is not the purpose of this book to speculate on the future of Amtrak and ConRail in terms of freight service. This chapter is simply a brief review of Amtrak freight-work equipment.

Alco road-switchers were always, in this writer's opinion, rather delightful looking and sounding locomotives. With graceful curves, the RS-3's gave the appearance of being able to handle any knd of a job, with or without snob appeal.Amtrak 126 and 133 (former New York Central 8254 and 8277) handle a Speno ballast cleaner work train near Harrisburg, Pennsylvania in electrified territory, Sept., 1977. (J.W. Swanberg)

Amtrak RS-3, No. 137 gently nudges a six car work train plus an ex-Pennsy caboose onto the double track main line and through a cross over at Shore Line Junction near New Haven in October, 1977. With the RS-3 and caboose simply stenciled "Amtrak," one cannot help but wonder what they will look like in full Amtrak dress. (J.W. Swanberg)

Conrail freight trains operate over Amtrak between Harrisburg and Washington, D.C. and Boston. This east-bound piggyback train is passing by the Colonia, New Jersey station on the four track main of the former Pennsylvania Railroad. (Harold Zabel)

With Amtrak ownership of the Northeast Corridor, much work was and is required to bring the track up to the former Pennsylvania Railroad standards of years ago. Through a special Federal loan and financial project, amounting to nearly $2 billion, the entire Corridor from Washington to Boston will be rebuilt permitting 120 miles per hour. In addition, electrifiction is planned for the New Haven-Boston segment of the district. (Amtrak)

Rebuilding the railroad is a complex operation. In this photo, crews are boring holes in ties and leading scrap metal into carts in preparation for the laying of new continuous welded rail.(Amtrak)

Before welded rail can be laid, cribbers must remove excess stone from between the ties to make space for rail anchors which will hold the new rail in place.(Amtrak)

In this photo a machine operator is running a "tie plug inserter". This machine inserts wooden plugs into the old spike holes, a job that must be completed before the welded rail is put in place.(Amtrak)

A Burro crane is used to set the welded rail onto the tie plates. (Amtrak)

Before the welded rail is spiked down, track crews use a Plasser spot tamper to raise and align portions of the track. It must be just right. (Amtrak)

Once the tie plates have been set, the rail laid and the holes bored, the spikes are set.(Amtrak)

Work Extra 779 West ambles along former Pennsy trackage near Colonia, New Jersey with five dump cars, one crane and a brightly painted orange Amtrak caboose. Other Amtrak freight and work equipment is also receiving orange paint. (Harold Zabel)

After the spikes have been set, crews use a spiking machine to hammer the spikes into the ties. Spiking machines are powered by a self-propelled air compressor operating directly behind the spiking operation. (Amtrak)

Probably the most interesting machine in Amtrak's Maintenance of Way equipment is this large track laying machine built by Canron Rail Group, Columbia, South Carolina. With 221 feet of length and weighing over 100 tons, the machine takes out the old rail and ties, plows away the ballast, lays down new ties and then places new continuous welded rail on top of the ties. This is completed in one operation at an averge speed of 1200 feet per hour.

Special tie cars, equipped with motorized portal gantries that run between the cars, are pushed ahead of the machine, which works equally well with concrete or timber ties. This is the first such machine in the United States. (Amtrak)

Chapter 9

Summary and Conclusions

The passenger train has a definite part to play in the future of North America. An energy short world, and immense problems with the highway and air systems, including overcrowding and excessive fuel useage dictate that the passenger train not be allowed to die. Amtrak must survive, either in the form of a government controlled corporation, or as a privately owned operator of train travel. The latter would not be unreasonable to expect, especially if the percentage of the rail share of inter-city travel would increase from the present 1% to 10%. The bus industry too would prosper with less automobile travel, and its financial problems would be alleviated. Further, there would be fewer automobile accidents and deaths, thereby still lowering the cost of travel in the U.S.A.

Another interesting point is that the crime rate too will drop as a result of less dependency on the automobile. Travel to and from crime sites would be less possible because of less access to automobiles. The problem can be solved. North America is not facing an impossible situation, but it will take some thinking, and some soul searching will be required by government leaders, the bus industry and even the railroads, themselves. It cannot be forgotten that the passenger train is a critical part of the nation's transportation economy, an economy that is not limitless in terms of resources, both physical and human. The next decade will tell the story, not only for the passenger train, but the entire transportation industry as well. It is not a question of whether or not we'll lose the passenger train, but rather a question of does the U.S.A. have the capacity and the fortitude to put together a balanced transportation system utilizing all modes effectively? If the Nation does not, the train will have to be re-invented at great expense. If it does, the U.S.A. will become a world leader in transportation. The resources are here to accomplish just that.

Amtrak recognizes the situation, and under the leadership of President Alan Boyd and the Board of Directors, the company is asking Congress to create a contract with Amtrak to run the rail passenger system. Congress would decide the basic level of service and Amtrak would run the trains at a specified cost. Amtrak would function essentially as an operating entity with Congress establishing basic structure and financing.

This recommendation was part of "Statement of Mission" which was made public at a press conference on December 13, 1978. The text of that statement is as follows:

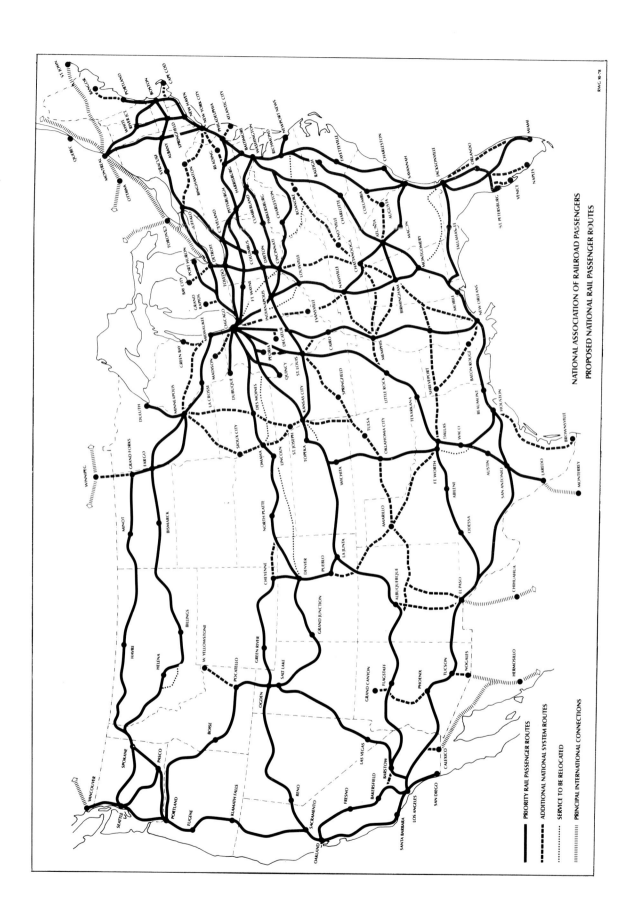

NATIONAL ASSOCIATION OF RAILROAD PASSENGERS
PROPOSED NATIONAL RAIL PASSENGER ROUTES

RWG. 10-78

PRIORITY RAIL PASSENGER ROUTES

ADDITIONAL NATIONAL SYSTEM ROUTES

SERVICE TO BE RELOCATED

PRINCIPAL INTERNATIONAL CONNECTIONS

The National Association of Railroad Passengers has published this map of recommended passenger train service throughout the United States. If such a net work were to be implemented, and co-ordinated with bus service and schedules, the U.S. would be well on its way to a balanced public passenger service as well as improving the overall energy consumption. (Map courtesy of National Association of Railroad Passengers)

The Lake Shore Limited is a prime example of successful route expansion and new services by Amtrak. Running since October, 1975, the New York-Boston -Chicago train has become very popular with travelers between Chicago and the Eastern Seaboard. The train now even requires a double unit dining car. This photo shows train 49 cruising through Chesterton, Indiana on Conrail's former New York Central trackage at about 40 miles per hour. Despite heavy snow fall in Northern Indiana on this February 3, 1979, the train is only a little off the time card. (Patrick C. Dorin).

THE AMTRAK MISSION STATEMENT
by Board of Directors, December 13, 1978

Introduction

The National Railroad Passenger Corporation, brought into being by Congress in 1970, was perceived by many different groups in many different ways.

Section 101 of the Rail Passenger Service Act (45 U.S.C. S 501) states that:

"The Congress finds that modern, efficient, intercity railroad passenger service is a necessary part of a balanced transportation system; that the public convenience and necessity require the continuance and improvement of such service to provide fast and comfortable transportation between crowded urban areas and in other areas of the country; that rail passenger service can help to end the congestion on our highways and the overcrowding of airways and airports; that the traveler in America should, to the maximum extent feasible, have freedom to choose the mode of travel most convenient to his needs; that to achieve these goals requires the designation of a basic national rail passenger system and the establishment of a Rail Passenger Corporation for the purpose of providing modern, efficient, intercity rail passenger service; that Federal financial assistance as well as investment capital from the private sector of the economy is needed for this purpose; and that interim emergency Federal financial assistance to certain railroads may be necessary to permit the orderly transfer of railroad passenger service to a Railroad Passenger Corporation."

During the ensuing eight years, much has been tried, much has been learned. Today, thanks to the Amtrak experience of the last several years, we as a Board can say with some confidence what the mission and purpose of Amtrak should be. With the value of hindsight, we conclude that a statement of mission would have been difficult, perhaps impossible, to articulate without first going through the experience of recent years. It is clear to the Board of Amtrak that the time has arrived when articulation of such a statement is not only desirable, but mandatory if Amtrak is to achieve its potential.

The statement that follows breaks into three broad parts. The first part deals with the major policy areas facing Amtrak and expresses the Board's view on what the solution should be to insure that Amtrak will be successful in serving the national interest. The second section outlines some persistent and major obstacles to the success of the Amtrak venture. These obstacles, although well known to Amtrak's Board and Management, have in the past been either misunderstood or ignored by the Congress, Executive Branch and the public at large. The final section indicates the Board's view as to why Amtrak merits continued public support.

A. The Major Policy Issues

The first part examines several major policy issues. The Board considers these issues to be of the highest priority but it does not consider this list to be exhaustive.

Routes

In Section 4(A) of the Amtrak Improvement Act of 1978, Congress has established the following five criteria to be used in developing route recommendations:

1. Unique characteristics of rail.
2. Energy conservation.
3. Relationship of benefits to cost.
4. Adequacy of alternative modes.
5. Market and population.

The Board has a responsibility to advise the Congress as to what it believes to be the optimum basic network.

Following the Congressional establishment of the basic network, the Board believes that Amtrak should be vested with authority to make additions to or deletions from the network and that it should employ as its criteria for such changes the "route criteria" developed by the Board in 1975 and approved by Congress. To the extent that existing Amtrak resources would permit adding service without need for specific further public funding, Amtrak should be empowered to do so. On the other hand, if additional public funding is necessary to commence such service, Amtrak should make explicit request to Congress for further appropriation by route, indicating the reasons for the request and detailing the criteria employed in reaching such conclusion.

All of the above should be done pursuant to the "contractual" approach outlined, in the following section.

Financing

There are only two sources of funds: fares and public financing. The Board believes the most effec-

176

tive method of handling public financing is through the establishment of a contractual relationship with Congress. Under such a system, the Board would operate the mandated **basic** system for an agreed-upon grant of funds. The level of funding would be determined taking into account expected costs of providing a quality product through an efficiently managed organization. This new form of contractual relationship would provide clear efficiency incentives to Amtrak and clear indications of management's performance to the Congress.

Productivity

The Board recognizes the public perception that rail labor may be less than fully productive. However, the issue is considerably more complicated than such a simple statement would suggest. In addition to the labor issue, part of the problem has to do with not-yet-entirely-corrected inefficiencies in management.

Some additional problems affecting productivity and cost control are:

1. Amtrak does not negotiate the terms and conditions of employment of the operating **craft** employees. The aim of Amtrak should be to develop a set of uniform terms and conditions for those persons who operate trains, but subject to the operating requirements of the contracting railroads.

2. Amtrak costs are inflated by protective guarantees to employees no longer working, as required by contract or law.

3. Productivity may be adversely affected by limited track access.

4. Productivity may be adversely affected by antiquated and restrictive work rules. These rules must be identified and eliminated.

5. Amtrak needs to develop a compensation system that is fair but one that permits efficient performance.

6. Amtrak needs more control over operations and should be a full party to all negotiations affecting Amtrak operations.

Commutation Service

The basic mission of Amtrak is to operate intercity rail passenger service. The provision of commuter service will degrade Amtrak's basic service. Should a public policy decision be made to impose commuter operations on Amtrak, compensation for the full costs must be provided.

U.S. Department of Transportation

The Department is in a difficult, if not impossible, position as both a member of the Amtrak Board and as an assigned agency of government exercising public oversight over budgetary and policy decisions. There is a strong sentiment on the Board that the Department of Transportation should not occupy a voting seat on the Amtrak Board. Others believe that despite what may be a conflict of interest, the Secretary of Transportation should retain a seat on the Board, as presently provided by law.

Congress

Historical approaches with regard to funding, route structure, levels of service, and the like, have contributed to a most difficult situation for the Congress. Very properly, members of Congress are concerned with both geographic and overall societal concerns. To improve this situation, the Board has made several recommendations under both routes and financing (above). If these recommendations are followed, Amtrak will essentially function as an operating entity with Congress establishing basic structure and financing.

Track

Poor Amtrak service is often directly attributable to poor track, usually caused by under maintenance and related slow orders. This problem falls into two broad classifications: (1) track that Amtrak owns; and (2) track belonging to certain contracting railroads.

1. The Northeast Corridor Improvement Project will provide good track, but the program now underway will not be completed for several years. Thus, public policy decisions relative to an important part of Amtrak operations have already been made, but expectations, particularly with regard to the timing of their impact, should be kept realistic. Moreover, additional funding may be required to complete the project.

2. With regard to track under control of contracting railroads, the issue is more difficult. Upgrading of such track requires substantial amounts of money not available to some railroads at this time. Such upgrading is a necessity if Amtrak is to provide effective service.

Equipment

Amtrak, from its inception, has had equipment problems. Much of the passenger equipment it acquired was old and sometimes badly maintained. Widespread shifts in equipment throughout the Amtrak system exacerbated the problem because many of the existing maintenance personnel were unfamiliar with the equipment that they were assigned to work on.

As Amtrak increasingly modernizes and standardizes its fleet, some of the present major maintenance problems will be reduced. Amtrak continues, however, to suffer from uneven quality of its maintenance facilities and, in some cases, poorly trained and inadequately supervised personnel.

A further major problem is the lack of a strong United States railroad passenger equipment supply industry. This places constraints upon Amtrak's ability to acquire new equipment and, more importantly, to develop new technology. Amtrak's equipment sitation would be appreciably improved if, as a matter of policy, the government gave better support to the development of new technology in the American industry or if, as a matter of policy, Amtrak was not constrained to buy only from an American supplier.

Obviously, Amtrak will need substantial capital to overcome equipment problems. The organization must develop a well-documented case to support requests for capital funding. Planning will preclude the necessity for frequent small capital requests and will enable both Amtrak management and the various branches of government to better appreciate the Amtrak capital plans in their proper, long-term context.

B. Obstacles

An enterprise for profit would typically be concerned with producing and selling a product. To do this, it must develop an organization with capability to design and efficiently produce the product to be vended. The product must attract sufficient customers to secure an adequate return to cover costs and a profit. By virtue of the public service nature of Amtrak, it cannot be held to this standard. Because of this, it is impossible to measure the efficiency of management by normal yardsticks.

Even without the market test, it is clear the purchasers of Amtrak services have not been satisfied. More correctly, the users, actual and potential, have been rightfully disappointed with the product supplied. By the same token, the vendors of services to Amtrak have not developed the respect for the organization which would induce them to put forth their best efforts.

Although the product deserves criticism, it should be understood that no management could avoid under existing circumstances substantial product failure. In the main, Amtrak inherited old equipment of diverse origin; it relies on a roadbed which has a large part of the system in bad repair; it inherited a work force trained in widely disparate operating procedures; it has undergone dramatic change in operating authority; it does not control substantial parts of its operations, and on and on.

All interested parties — consumers, employees, management, D.O.T., Congress, and equipment suppliers — have been disappointed Amtrak has not lived up to expectations and has not captured as large a portion of the market as could have been expected.

Amtrak internally is facing management problems. Highly qualified personnel are often beyond reach because of compensation limits. Morale is undermined because of Amtrak's uncertain future

and manifold operating difficulties, many of which are beyond Amtrak's control.

A major operating difficulty has been Amtrak's inheritance of old, obsolete, and badly maintained passenger equipment. In trying to keep its cars in operation, including diners and sleeping cars in short supply, Amtrak at first relied upon contracting railroads for maintenance, but it gradually assumed this function itself, acquiring old railroad facilities manned by railroad personnel. This takeover program had more than its share of start-up problems and only slowly is a coordinated maintenance program beginning to emerge. The maintenance of air-conditioning equipment has been a special problem, and progress has been exasperatingly slow. The introduction of new equipment, headend power, and modern air-conditioning equipment for installation in the older cars will help.

A clear and understandable fare policy for Amtrak does not exist. This is of special importance because Amtrak is free of all economic regulation in fixing its prices. The marketing function must be developed to the point where the separate and distinct conditions in the several Amtrak operating regions can be dealt with realistically in providing and pricing its services.

Amtrak must improve its credibility in dealing with Congress and public authorities and respond positively to criticism in the press and from the public. This task is complicated by the fact that, in many circumstances, poor service on Amtrak trains is directly traceable to the contracting railroads.It is essential that these railroads acquire and maintain a sense of Amtrak's mission in developing rail passenger transportation service for the country.

As noted above, Amtrak will face a number of critical problems in the near term, and the ultimate resolution of these problems will plainly determine the future of the organization. If the present situation persists without substantial improvement, there is no reason to believe that Amtrak will survive for much longer in its present form.

Some have contended that the problems currently facing the organization are so grave as to actually threaten the survival of intercity rail passenger transportaion in the United States. However, given the fact that rail transportation will, for a long while to come, remain as a strong alternative mode of transportation (due to potential fuel economics, speed, convenience, and comfort), it is unlikely that intercity rail passenger transportation will fail to survive. Rather, it is more likely that Amtrak will be "nationalized" if it is unable to improve on existing operations.

However, the nationalization of Amtrak surely is no panacea for the problems inherent in the organization. For one thing, there is no reason to believe that Amtrak will run better under the weight of yet another federal bureaucracy. For another thing, the plain truth is that no intercity rail passenger system will ever fully capture the potential market in this country until we cure problems associated with poor track, obsolete equipment, inadequate funding, and the like. As noted above, an intercity rail system is a public service and not a for-profit operation. Once this fact is recognized, and once some serious political judgments are made with respect to the nature of the service to be provided to the American public, then funding levels can be realistically established. If and when funding is fixed to achieve a realistic service goal, then and only then will Amtrak be able to chart a meaningful course for the future.

C. Conclusion

Precise measurements of the value of any public service are difficult to achieve; this is true with Amtrak. There are real and substantial public benefits that acrue from the operation of Amtrak.

Increasing congestion in the air and highway modes is a fact. Amtrak does serve to alleviate this problem, particularly in, but not limited to the Northeast Corridor. This alone emphasizes the importance of providing the travelling public with a choice of modes.

Allied to the provision of relieving congestion is the major benefit that railroad right-of-way, with its enormous capacity, saves from the alternate consumption of land to serve other modes. An additional value is the undisputed potential available for energy efficiency associated with increased utilization of rail passenger transportation.

Also, in the mind of this Board, there is no doubt that in time of national emergency the services and facilities of a nationwide rail passenger service would be called upon to support the national security.

Last, but not least, rail passenger service is acknowledged to be the safest way to travel; it will remain so. For this and other reasons, there is a clearly expressed national desire to maintain a national rail passenger service. There is a sense of national pride which desires that service to be of superior quality.

Source: Amtrak, Washington, D.C., December 13, 1978.

Such a contract with Congress would serve to solve many of the problems of Amtrak, and would finally put the Nation on the way to a balanced transportation system. The next two years of 1979 and 1980 will be crucial ones for Amtrak and the railroad industry as a whole. If congress, the Department of Transportation, the various states and the railroad industry cooperate with each other and with Amtrak, such a contract will not only be able to be created between Amtrak and Congress, but also will be fulfilled. The benefits would be far reaching and perhaps passenger service would be placed in operation to the many cities and towns throughout the United States that are now without safe, all weather transportation. The bus industry too will benefit. The contract with Congress is, at this time, the only logical alternative.

Epilogue

In January, 1979, Transportation Secretary Brock Adams released the Department of Transportation's report recommending substantial cut backs in train service throughout the United States. This report was released to the United States and recommended to Congress despite the fact that the Nation is faced with an energy crisis, that the Nation is actually subsidizing air passengers at an even greater rate than Amtrak rail passengers and that highway repair and construction costs are soaring out of sight. The recommendation was made in spite of the fact that the rail system could provide the Nation with the most economical system for moving large numbers of people in comfort and safety at speeds in excess of 100 miles per hour. As written in Chapter 1, the Japanese investigated air, rail and highway modes and found the rail system to be most attractive in terms of economics and environmental impact.

It is difficult to predict what Congress will do with the DOT report. However as this is being written, the crisis in Iran is already causing government leaders, both state and federal, to be predicting problems at the gasoline stations in the near future. The sad part of the story is that the U.S. is now (in 1979) even more dependent upon the Mid-East for oil than during the last crisis in 1973. Instead of solving the problem internally by revamping our transportation system, and rebuilding the rail system, the Nation has chosen to buy even more foreign oil. This in turn has increased the inflation rate, allowed foreign control or at least major purchases of American businesses and farm land, which in turn has caused a very weak U.S. dollar. Congress must simply take into consideration all of these problems. Hopefully, Congress will reject the DOT report and by the time this book is in print, Amtrak will be on a more solid footing.

Amtrak responded to the DOT report with a News Release on January 31, 1979. The text of that release is as follows:

"WASHINGTON, D.C.—'What is it worth to America to acquire and maintain benefits which are generated by a rail passenger transportation system?'

That's the primary question Amtrak believe has to be answered following the release today of the U.S. Department of Transportation plan to restructure the Amtrak system.

In an "Amtrak Perspective" on the DOT Report, the corporation said that 'the question of what specific routes are to be operated will always be subjective regardless of the efforts made to describe and define economic and social criteria' and after seven-and-a-half years of experience 'there is no statistical method whereby an optimal rail network can be established.'

Amtrak concluded, therefore, 'the issues are not resolved initially by a map,' but by deciding the key policy issues relating to the benefits and costs of a rail passenger system in context with the nation's total transportation needs.'

On the benefits side, the Amtrak Board of Directors believes there are clear and substantial arguments for a rail passenger system. They are:

•Availability of an intercity mass transit mode for those who cannot or choose not to travel by other means.
•Environmental aspects of land use, air and noise pollution.
•Potential energy savings through efficiency, especially since railroad energy consumption is or can be, derived from energy sources other than imported oil.

•Availability of the safest mode of travel.
•Provision of city-center service which in turn promotes economic development including intermodal facilities.

Amtrak acknowledged that while these benefits can be identified, some are difficult to quantify. And they must be purchased at a cost.

'Experience shows that rail passenger services in the U.S. and in all major countries of the world are not capable of operating solely on the income from commercial revenues,' said Amtrak's statement. 'Social benefits are an integral but not easily quantifiable element.'

The Corporation, which said it will be 'fully responsive to the requests of Congress for information and assistance as it develops its views on the future of Amtrak,' released a list of concerns regarding DOT's recommendations.

Issues raised include level of service over routes; future usage of tracks owned by private railroads; lack of management flexibility; operating and cost problems in making the transition to a new route structure; cost reimbursement for providing commuter rail service; and Amtrak's role in national emergencies.

Level of Service

Amtrak said its problems are largely due to the fact that limited service is being maintained over too large a system without adequate resources.

'The Amtrak Board believes that the route restructuring process is essential. However, if it leads to still inadequate service operated over a smaller system, then the public will not be well served,' said the statement.

Future Use

The Corporation said its trains operate by virtue of contracts between Amtrak and private railroads that own most lines, and changes in train routings could affect future operations.

'To the extent the current route system is reduced, the contractual obligations of the railroads no longer providing passenger service will be lost. The net effect of this is clear: those railroads will no longer be required to maintain their physical plant at the elevated level of condition necessary to operate a rail passenger system,' said Amtrak.

It is suggested that in any route reduction, funding to maintain currently used facilities in a standby state of readiness should be considered.

Management Flexibility

Amtrak said it is a management function to determine train frequencies, routings, on-board service, equipment usage, schedules and fares according to its legislative mandate.

In the DOT report, however, the system recommended in conjunction with the funding provided effectively eliminates that flexibility.

'For example, the Amtrak Board has adopted a policy that daily train service is the minimum service that should be offered the traveling public. The report recommends tri-weekly service over some routes,' said Amtrak.

Transition to Recommended Routes

Should DOT's report be accepted by Congress, Amtrak is expected to change routes Oct. 1. But, Amtrak said, 'The report overlooks the real possibility that not all railroads will be in position to permit operation of proposed routes on the schedules assumed or at the cost levels contained in the funding. The need for track connections and other modifications require unavoidable lead time in many instances.'

Amtrak said this raises a possible funding problem in connection with continuing service on existing routes designated for abandonment pending the completion of necessary construction on the proposed restructured routes.

Commuter Services

Amtrak urged that the economics of commuter rail service be realistically addressed. Since the recent change in law authorizing Amtrak to operate commuter trains, several state and regional agencies have shown interest in Amtrak undertaking such service.

It is strongly believed by Amtrak that full reimbursement for total costs must be provided for it to enter into commuter rail contracts.

National Emergencies

The DOT report was not required to consider the extent to which, if at all, railroad passenger service is required in a national emergency. Amtrak's Board pointed out in its Mission Statement released in December that this is a point which could be properly addressed by Congress in considering a revised route structure.

Contractual Relationship Proposed

Amtrak said it is prepared to propose a refined set of standards or criteria against which its operation should be measured and through which future route alignments could be considered.

This coincides with the Amtrak Board of Director's belief, as announced in December, that the most effective method of handling public financing of Amtrak is through establishment of a 'contractual relationship' with Congress. Amtrak supported DOT's recommendation for long-term authorization as an essential element of this relationship."

End of text of news release.

Although Amtrak has recommended that a contract be established with Congress, the recommendation does not really go far enough. However, realistically, Amtrak may not have the power to go further with its recommendations during this particular period with the current political climate.

The writer feels that a several step process should be undertaken to solve the transportation and energy crisis the United States is currently facing.

First, both Amtrak and the individual railroads, as well as the bus companies, should receive appropriate financing to purchase new passenger equipment and buses on a large scale.

Secondly, this purchase should be in line with new Federal guidelines for a transportation policy and an immediate reduction in the amount of crude oil imported from foreign countries. This could be handled by a planned reduction in purchases, such as 5 to 10% per year while at the same time the various bus companies and railroads would be able to provide public transportation service on an expanding scale to compensate for the fewer gallons of gasoline that would be available. This would mean not only long haul passenger service, but also suburban and intraurban services. This method or plan of gradual change would continue until 90% or more of U.S. dependence on foreign oils would be eliminated.

A third part of the plan would be to insure that rural residents would have sufficient gasoline to be able to drive to park n'ride facilities. If people were unable to travel to public transport stations, the overall plan would have little value.

The railroads would be capable of handling such increases in passenger train service. During the 1920's, many rail lines handled substantially more train traffic than one finds in the 1970's. Perhaps some lines would need to be double or triple tracked, but the traffic could be handled. Perhaps, some railroad lines will need to be put back into service. The writer is thinking about some of the Conrail lines that have been discontinued that were once fine main lines under the direction of the Lehigh Valley, the Erie and others. Although one has to admit that the fine maintenance described was discontinued by some of those railroads shortly after World War II.

In closing, the writer feels that the railroads—under private ownership—would be quite capable of handling the passenger loads necessary to reduce our dependence on foreign oils. However, a National Transportation Policy is needed, and it is needed soon before disaster strikes. If such a plan were to be put in operation, there would be no need to worry about enough heating oil for homes, schools, hospitals and businesses. The railroads have the power to rescue the Nation from the energy crisis.

The railroad companies too must be far more positive about the situation. Negative comments by a company explaining that there is no room for passenger trains, look mighty silly when the same company says they have the capacity for other types of trains. Further negative comments by railroad personnel, especially at the senior management levels, only makes the public think that the railroads are a dying business.

A big job must be done if the U.S. is to avoid a real crisis. The time to start is now. The Nation cannot wait much longer. Let us hope that sound thinking will prevail.

Special Note: As we go to press, the future of many Amtrak routes has still not been decided by Congress or the D.O.T.. One encouraging point, additional bus and rail cooperative routings and connections have been established nationwide.

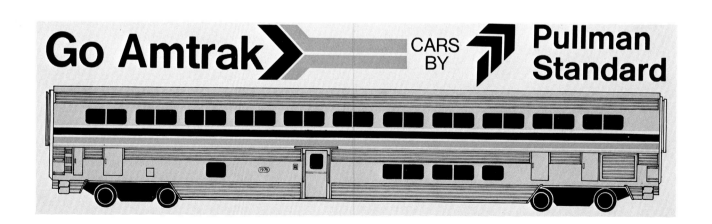

BIBLIOGRAPHY

Chapter 1

1 "Intercity Buses Found Most Fuel Efficient and Least Polluting in Study," *Traffic World,* June 5,1978, p. 18.
2 "Relative Fuel Efficiency," Amtrak, April, 1978.
3 "Background on Amtrak," Amtrak, 1977, p. 24.
4 Harry L. Tennant, "Bus Companies Rip Amtrak on Funds," *Modern Railroads,* June, 1978, p.35.
5 Adriana Gianturce, Director of California Department of Transportation, Regarding Proposed Cuts in Amtrak Service in California, May 11, 1978.
6 "Background on Amtrak," Amtrak, 1978.
7 D. Philip Locklin, *Economics of Transportation,* Homewood, Illinois: Richard D. Irwin, Inc. Fourth Edition, 1954, p. 118.
8 Harry L. Tennant, *op. cit.,* p. 35.
9 Garth Campbell, Addressing the National Association of Railroad Passengers.
10 Adriana Gianturce, See footnote No. 5.
11 Transportation Committee Meetings, East Central Regional Development Council of Minnesota, Mora, Minnesota, 1978.
12 "Background on Amtrak," 1977.

Chapters 2, 3, 4, 5, 6, 7, 8 and 9

Amtrak Annual Reports, 1973, 1974, 1975, 1976, 1977 and 1978.
"Background on Amtrak," 1973, 1977.
Amtrak Passenger Train Time Tables, 1971 through 1978.
Amtrak Features, Washington, D.C.: National Railroad Passenger Corporation, December, 1974, p. 1.
Amtrak, *News Releases,* June, 1971 through February, 1979.
Amtrak News, A Newsletter for Amtrak Employees, 1974 through 1978.
Amtrak Mission Statement, Washington, D.C., December 13, 1978.